FT Prentice Hall
FINANCIAL TIMES

In an increasingly competitive world, we believe it's quality of thinking that gives you the edge – an idea that opens new doors, a technique that solves a problem or an insight that simply makes sense of it all. The more you know, the smarter and faster you can go.

That's why we work with the best minds in business and finance to bring cutting-edge thinking and best learning practice to a global market.

Under a range of leading imprints, including *Financial Times Prentice Hall*, we create world-class print publications and electronic products bringing our readers knowledge, skills and understanding, which can be applied whether studying or at work.

To find out more about Pearson Education publications or tell us about the books you'd like to find, you can visit us at **www.pearsoned.co.uk**

FAST TRACK TO SUCCESS
MARKETING

CHRIS RITCHIE

An imprint of **Pearson Education**

Harlow, England • London • New York • Boston • San Francisco • Toronto • Sydney • Singapore • Hong Kong
Tokyo • Seoul • Taipei • New Delhi • Cape Town • Madrid • Mexico City • Amsterdam • Munich • Paris • Milan

PEARSON EDUCATION LIMITED

Edinburgh Gate
Harlow CM20 2JE
Tel: +44 (0)1279 623623
Fax: +44 (0)1279 431059
Website: www.pearsoned.co.uk

First published in Great Britain in 2009

© Pearson Education Limited 2009

ISBN: 978-0-273-72180-2

British Library Cataloguing-in-Publication Data
A catalogue record for this book is available from the British Library

Library of Congress Cataloging-in-Publication Data
Ritchie, Chris, 1962-
  Marketing / Chris Ritchie.
    p. cm. -- (Fast track to success)
  Includes bibliographical references and index.
  ISBN 978-0-273-72180-2 (pbk. : alk. paper) 1. Marketing--Management.
  2. Marketing. I. Title.
  HF5415.13.R49 2009
  658.8--dc22
                            2009009843

10 9 8 7 6 5 4 3 2 1
13 12 11 10 09

Series text design by Design Deluxe
Typeset in 10/15 Swis Lt by 30
Printed by Ashford Colour Press Ltd, Gosport

The publisher's policy is to use paper manufactured from sustainable forests.

CONTENTS

THE FAST TRACK WAY

Everything you need to accelerate your career

The best way to fast track your career as a manager is to fast track the contribution you and your team make to your organisation and for your team to be successful in as public a way as possible. That's what the Fast Track series is about. The Fast Track manager delivers against performance expectations, is personally highly effective and efficient, develops the full potential of their team, is recognised as a key opinion leader in the business, and ultimately progresses up the organisation ahead of their peers.

You will benefit from the books in the Fast Track series whether you are an ambitious first-time team leader or a more experienced manager who is keen to develop further over the next few years. You may be a specialist aiming to master every aspect of your chosen discipline or function, or simply be trying to broaden your awareness of other key management disciplines and skills. In either case, you will have the motivation to critically review yourself and your team using the tools and techniques presented in this book, as well as the time to stop, think and act on areas you identify for improvement.

Do you know what you need to know and do to make a real difference to your performance at work, your contribution to your company and your blossoming career? For most of us, the honest answer is 'Not really, no'. It's not surprising then that most of us never reach our full potential. The innovative Fast Track series gives you exactly what you need to speed up your progress and become a high performance manager in all the areas of the business that matter. Fast Track is not just another 'How to' series. Books on selling tell you how to win sales but not how to move from salesperson to sales manager. Project management software enables you to plan detailed tasks but doesn't improve the quality of your project management thinking and business performance. A marketing book tells you about the principles of marketing but not how to lead a team of marketers. It's not enough.

Specially designed features in the Fast Track books will help you to see what you need to know and to develop the skills you need to be successful. They give you:

→ the information required for you to shine in your chosen function or skill – particularly in the Fast Track top ten;

→ practical advice in the form of Quick Tips and answers to FAQs from people who have been there before you and succeeded;

→ state of the art best practice as explained by today's academics and industry experts in specially written Expert Voices;

→ case stories and examples of what works and, perhaps more importantly, what doesn't work;

→ comprehensive tools for accelerating the effectiveness and performance of your team;

→ a framework that helps you to develop your career as well as produce terrific results.

Fast Track is a resource of business thinking, approaches and techniques presented in a variety of ways – in short, a complete performance support environment. It enables managers to build careers from their first tentative steps into management all the way up to becoming a business director – accelerating the performance of their team and their career. When you use the Fast Track approach with your team it provides a common business language and structure, based on best business practice. You will benefit from the book whether or not others in the organisation adopt the same practices; indeed if they don't, it will give you an edge over them. Each Fast Track book blends hard practical advice from expert practitioners with insights and the latest thinking from experts from leading business schools.

The Fast Track approach will be valuable to team leaders and managers from all industry sectors and functional areas. It is for ambitious people who have already acquired some team leadership skills and have realised just how much more there is to know.

If you want to progress further you will be directed towards additional learning and development resources via an interactive Fast Track website, **www.Fast-Track-Me.com**. For many, these books therefore become the first step in a journey of continuous development. So, the Fast Track approach gives you everything you need to accelerate your career, offering you the opportunity to develop your knowledge and skills, improve your team's performance, benefit your organisation's progress towards its aims and light the fuse under your true career potential.

ABOUT THE AUTHOR

CHRIS RITCHIE is a marketing professional with almost 25 years' experience in a wide variety of sales and marketing roles covering most of the marketing spectrum. While much of that experience was gained in the technology industry, he has also worked in a wide range of other sectors, including sports marketing, the public sector, financial services, manufacturing, the food industry and professional services (including training and management consulting).

After many years in corporate life, Chris is now a director of two marketing businesses focused on driving revenue and building relationships for their clients. Sine Qua Non International focuses on experiential marketing, particularly sponsorships and sports, while Collumbell Communications offers marketing services to the technology sector. Together they share a common capability centred on the development and execution of marketing, PR, and event and hospitality programmes. Clients have included SanDisk, Hitachi, Accenture, Imation, Avaya, Ducati, Dorna, Attenda, SmartTrust, AOMi and Sun Microsystems.

Chris received a BSc (Hons) at the University College of Wales, Aberystwyth, in 1984 and an MBA from the University of Warwick in 1995.

Chris Ritchie, Sine Qua Non International Ltd,
Chiltern House, 45 Station Road, Henley-on-Thames,
Oxfordshire, RG9 1AT, UK
E chris.ritchie@sinequanon-intl.com
T 00 44 (0) 1491 845 420
W www.sinequanon-intl.com

A WORD OF THANKS FROM THE AUTHOR

I would like to thank the following for their generous contributions to this book.

→ **Liz Gooster, Pearson.** There are many exciting new ideas in the publishing world at present, but without an enthusiastic champion, most will simply die a slow death. Liz had the confidence to commission the Fast Track series and associated web-tool on behalf of the Pearson Group at a time when other publishers were cutting back on non-core activities. She has remained committed to its success – providing direction, challenge and encouragement as and when required.

→ **Ken Langdon.** As well as being a leading author in his own right, Ken has worked with all the Fast Track authors to bring a degree of rigour and consistency to the series. As each book has developed, he has been a driving force behind the scenes, pulling the detailed content for each title together in the background – working with an equal measure of enthusiasm and patience!

→ **Mollie Dickenson.** Mollie has a background in publishing and works as a research manager at Henley Business School, and has been a supporter of the project from its inception. She has provided constant encouragement and challenge, and is, as always, an absolute delight to work with.

→ **Critical readers.** As the Fast Track series evolved, it was vital that we received constant challenge and input from other experts and from critical readers.

→ **Professor David Birchall.** David has worked to identify and source Expert Voice contributions from international academic and business experts in each Fast Track title. David is co-author of the Fast Track *Innovation* book and a leading academic author in his own right, and has spent much of the last 20 years heading up the research programme at Henley Business School – one of the world's top ten business schools.

Our expert team

Last but not least, I am grateful for the contributions made by experts from around the world in each of the Fast Track titles.

EXPERT	TOPIC	BUSINESS SCHOOL/ COMPANY
Professor Jean-Jacques Chanaron	Positioning marketing in the innovation process (p. 18)	Grenoble Ecole de Management, France
Professor Caroline Tynan	Service-dominant logic (p. 28)	Nottingham University Business School, University of Nottingham
Practice Associate Professor John A. Davis	Successful brand building means evoking history – the case of the Olympic Games (p. 63)	Lee Kong Chian School of Business, Singapore Management University, Singapore
Cigdem Gogus	Mobile marketing – an up-close and interactive way to market (p. 83)	Henley Business School, University of Reading
Professor David Birchall	New product development – paying attention to critical decisions (p. 98)	Henley Business School, University of Reading
Professor Douglas West	Key trends in advertising (p. 126)	Birmingham Business School, University of Birmingham, and Editor, *International Journal of Advertising*
Professor John Roberts and Pamela Morrison	Measuring is good; measuring what matters might be even better (p. 150)	Australian School of Business, University of New South Wales, Australia
Paul Gostick	Marketers must step up to the mark (p. 165)	Chairman, Chartered Institute of Marketing, 2004–8

PUBLISHER'S ACKNOWLEDGEMENTS

We are grateful to the following for permission to reproduce copyright material:

Figures

Figure on page 41 adapted from 'Strategies of Diversification', *Harvard Business Review*, 25(5), 113–25 (Ansoff, I., Sept/Oct 1957); Figure on page 49 from The Growth Share Matrix – The Star, the Dog, the Cow and the Question Mark (Boston Consulting Group, 1970), THE BCG PORT-FOLIO MATRIX from the PRODUCT PORTFOLIO MATRIX, © 1970, THE BOSTON CONSULTING GROUP; Figure on page 188 adapted from 'How competitive forces shape strategy', *Harvard Business Review*, March/April (Porter, M., 1979).

Text

Plan template on pages 179–80 from *Marketing Plans: How to Prepare Them, How to Use Them*, 6th ed., Butterworth-Heinemann (McDonald, M., 2007). Reproduced with permission of the author.

In some instances we have been unable to trace the owners of copyright material, and we would appreciate any information that would enable us to do so.

MARKETING FAST TRACK

Marketing is all about relationships – relationships with the client, with the brand, with media and with colleagues. The marketing strategy is the absolute hub of the business and therefore to some extent has to embrace every part of that business. Each part of the business should input something to that strategy because everyone is affected by that strategy: from R&D to production and from finance through sales to HR. Marketing is not about sitting back and wondering at the splendour of a brilliantly conceived ad campaign – the real role of marketing is to pull together the inputs of everybody involved (and everybody is involved) and then to get everyone to buy into the implementation of that strategy. To make that work, the Fast Track marketer must successfully address both the internal audience and the external audience.

Of all these relationships, the relationship with the customer is still king. True marketing successes, as demonstrated by companies such as Apple and Red Bull, go beyond the product and create a customer relationship with the company itself. The result of that is that people will continue to buy from that company even if the product is perceived to be the same, or perhaps slightly worse than the latest offering from a competitor. To achieve that, the company itself must be seen to stand for something – a set of expectations it will deliver to its customers. John Lewis, the well-known UK department store, is a good example of this, with its ethical employment policies and 'never knowingly undersold' price promise. Traditionally McDonald's offers a very different set of expectations to John Lewis, but it nonetheless meets them and does so consistently. In very different ways both companies engage the customer with the company more than with the product. To do that, the business needs to align and integrate their people, their processes and their promises to create the experience. Marketing should play a central role in defining and ensuring the delivery of that experience.

What was once called 'customer satisfaction' has now evolved into the idea of the 'customer experience' – and that experience lies at the heart of marketing. Problems arise when the marketing messages directed at the internal audience don't match those directed at the external consumers. The result is a disconnect between what customers are told and what they experience; a disconnect that can be boiled down to the all too familiar example of: 'Your business is important to us … the wait time to speak to someone is seven minutes.'

My mobile phone company once sent me a letter from credit control saying that my account was suspended because my direct debit had been refused and that I was to call the following number to avoid reconnection charges. So I did, only to be told that I had the wrong number because I was listed under 'business' and this service was for 'residential' – and, no, they couldn't put me through. So I had to ring another number instead. The number turned out to be invalid. Tension mounting, I called back and got another operator, who this time had no problem putting me through to the right number. That was when I finally found that there was no problem with the account in the first place. An isolated incident? Perhaps, but then again the same type of frustrations arose when I wanted to transfer from one contract to another – I was repeatedly told I couldn't, until it was accepted that I could. During all this time I continued to receive flyers and marketing messages selling me new products and telling me about how wonderful the service was.

If you strip away the frustration and examine the logic of what was going wrong here, we have a classic example of the marketing disconnect. The company was simply not listening to me because it was working in thick-walled silos – each function had its own processes developed without regard for what I needed or wanted. This clearly included marketing, which was relegated to pushing new products at me. In terms of my experience, these new promises came in pretty much the same breath as the one from customer services telling me to get lost. Service agents were not empowered or trained or capable enough to deliver and follow through on the promise. The marketing message and the customer experience did not match up.

Little about this story will surprise anyone with a mobile phone, yet the lesson to be learnt could not be clearer. Marketing must be involved with the delivery of the experience – if it isn't, then the business will suffer. Marketing must explore the capabilities of the organisation and match them accurately with the expectations of the customer. Expectations of phone companies are pretty low across the board, but to the Fast Track marketer this kind of disconnect should leap out as an outstanding opportunity.

This 'holistic' approach to marketing – from worker through product to customer – inevitably involves a larger picture, which means this book has a broad scope. That doesn't mean you have to take it all in at once. Instead, see it as a combination of atlas and roadmap – the big picture is there for you but so are the directions and shortcuts to fast track you to where you want to go.

HOW TO USE THIS BOOK

Fast Track books present a collection of the latest tools, techniques and advice to help build your team and your career. Use this table to plan your route through the book.

PART	OVERVIEW
About the author	A brief overview of the author, his background and his contact details
A **Awareness**	*This first part gives you an opportunity to gain a quick overview of the topic and to reflect on your current effectiveness*
1 *Marketing in a nutshell*	A brief overview of marketing and a series of frequently asked questions to bring you up to speed quickly
2 *Marketing audit*	Simple checklists to help identify strengths and weaknesses in your team and your capabilities
B **Business Fast Track**	*Part B provides tools and techniques that may form part of the marketing framework for you and your team*
3 *Fast Track top ten*	Ten tools and techniques to help you implement a sustainable approach to marketing based on the latest best practice
4 *Technologies*	A review of the latest technologies used to improve effectiveness and efficiency of marketing activities
5 *Implementing change*	A detailed checklist to identify gaps and to plan the changes necessary to implement your marketing framework
C **Career Fast Track**	*Part C focuses on you, your leadership qualities and what it takes to get to the top*
6 *The first ten weeks*	Recommended activities when starting a new role in marketing, together with a checklist of useful facts to know
7 *Leading the team*	Managing change, building your team and deciding your leadership style
8 *Getting to the top*	Becoming a marketing professional, getting promoted and becoming a director – what does it take?
D **Director's toolkit**	*The final part provides more advanced tools and techniques based on industry best practice*
Toolkit	Advanced tools and techniques used by senior managers
Glossary	Glossary of terms

FAST-TRACK-ME.COM

Throughout this book you will be encouraged to make use of the companion site: **www.Fast-Track-Me.com**. This is a custom-designed, highly interactive online resource that addresses the needs of the busy manager by providing access to ideas and methods that will improve individual and team performance quickly. Top features include:

→ **Health Checks.** Self-audit checklists allowing evaluation of you and your team against industry criteria. You will be able to identify areas of concern and plan for their resolution using a personal 'Get-2-Green' action plan.

→ **The Knowledge Cube.** The K-Cube is a two-dimensional matrix presenting Fast Track features from all topics in a consistent and easy-to-use way – providing ideas, tools and techniques in a single place, anytime, anywhere. This is a great way to delve in and out of business topics quickly.

→ **The Online Coach.** The Online Coach is a toolkit of fully interactive business templates in MS Word format that allow Fast-Track-Me.com users to explore specific business methods (strategy, ideas, projects etc.) and learn from concepts, case examples and other resources according to your preferred learning style.

→ **Business Glossary.** The Fast Track Business Glossary provides a comprehensive list of key words associated with each title in the Fast Track series, together with a plain English definition – helping you to cut through business jargon.

The website can also help answer some of the vital questions managers are asking themselves today (see figure overleaf).

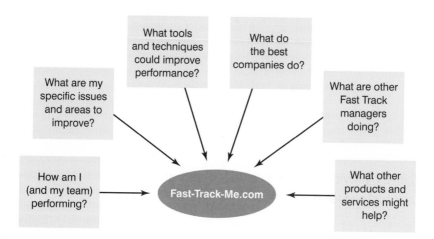

Don't get left behind: log on to **www.Fast-Track-Me.com** now to get your career on the fast track.

PART A

AWARENESS

This book introduces a sustainable approach to marketing aimed at keeping you, your team and your organisation at the forefront of the process, thus contributing towards the future of all three. The starting point is to gain a quick understanding of what marketing is and what it is not, and to be aware of your and your team's capabilities in this area right now. You will need to ask yourself a number of questions that will reveal where you and your team need to improve if you are to drive a true marketing orientation within the business: creating offerings that are sought out by customers and admired and respected by your industry competitors.

'Know yourself' was the motto above the doorway of the Oracle at Delphi and is a wise thought. It means that you must do an open and honest self-audit as you start on the process of setting up your marketing framework.

The stakes are high. Marketing is at the heart of success in this global, competitive marketplace. Your team, therefore, need to be effective marketers and you need to be a good leader. Poor leadership and poor team effectiveness will make failure likely. An effective team poorly led will sap the team's energy and lead in the long term to failure through their leaving for a better environment or becoming less effective through lack of motivation. Leading an ineffective team well is unlikely to get you much credit unless you can turn things round and improve the team performance. So, looking at the figure below, how do you make sure that you and your team are in the top right-hand box – an effective team with an excellent leader? That's what this book is about, and this section shows you how to discover your and your team's starting point.

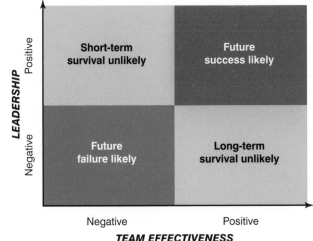

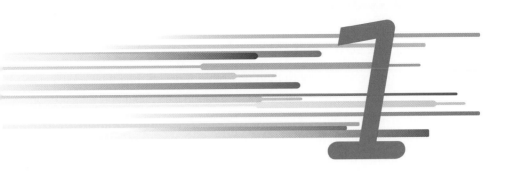

MARKETING IN A NUTSHELL

Starting with the basics

Just what is marketing?

One of the most misunderstood business functions, marketing represents different things to different people. Some people think that it's about the promotional activities that support the sales function in generating revenue and convincing customers to buy products and services. The danger of this view is that it can lead to tactical, disjointed activities that try to stimulate sales through short-term promotion and communications. Others emphasise the product marketing and product development aspects of defining and pricing products in competitive markets, an approach that can result in companies forever chasing the Holy Grail of the 'better mousetrap'. Others still equate marketing with above-the-line advertising, which continues to pervade everyday life, particularly with the explosion of media channels. Sponsorship and PR are other powerful marketing variants, but only come into their own as part of a wider, integrated approach.

In reality marketing is all this and more. It's about identifying market opportunities for products and services that customers want or need, and coordinating internal and external resources to deliver those services with a healthy margin. It's also about communicating and engaging with target prospective customers to position your company's offerings in their consciousness.

Why is it so important?

Marketing, possibly more than any other function, has the capability to dramatically transform the business through integrated and effective tactical activity. It is probably the defining success factor for today's businesses. Try to draw up a list of the businesses you admire most and see if there's a single one among them that doesn't excel at marketing!

Gone are the days when organisations could thrive solely on the basis of good products at keen prices. Today, marketing is what produces market leaders – companies with clearly differentiated customer experiences, strong margins and the ability to promote themselves with a compelling story and engaging experience.

This evolution in the importance and complexity of marketing has coincided with three major trends:

1 **Customer or buyer power is increasing as a result of easier access to vast sources of information.** The internet initially enabled customers to browse and compare features and prices in an efficient manner, but that was just the start. The rise of social networking, peer-to-peer networks and viral marketing means that customers and prospects are exchanging positive and negative messages about your offering across cyber space – and out of your control. In parallel, your customers' expectations of their experiences are rising, not only of the purchase and product, but also of the level and quality of your engagement with them. When word of mouth was the norm the story goes that a satisfied customer would tell three people, while a disgruntled customer shouts to ten. Those figures can now be multiplied by millions. Your point of control now is in delivering the experience.

2 **Globalisation combines two trends in one.** Large, market-leading companies are consolidating markets on a global basis, buying up smaller local or international competitors and adding to market share and influence. At the same time companies from emerging economies with low-wage structures, such as India, China and Brazil, are able to access local markets around the world. The internet and other high-tech communications

advances, together with highly efficient global and local distribution networks, mean that almost any business is now able to access any chosen market.

3 **These two trends combine with advances in product development and technology and customer expectations for new solutions to continually shorten product life cycles.** The marketing department is now faced with an ever smaller window of opportunity to establish a market position and turn a profit before that product, or to a lesser extent service, becomes obsolete. This applies beyond products to entire product categories. In the 1970s VHS video took several years to establish market dominance over Betamax. In 2008 the Blue-Ray disk format overhauled HD-DVD, in effect before either technology had even made any impact on the mass market.

Marketing and innovation have become inextricably linked. Companies need to differentiate themselves and their propositions, and the only way to do that is through innovation – whether in the core product, the service, the overall experience or in the way those factors are marketed.

So why is marketing difficult – what typically goes wrong?

Marketing is crucial, but it's not as easy as people sometimes think and unfortunately things can and do go wrong. Consider each of the following potential pitfalls and identify which might apply to you, your team and your organisation, and then think what you can do about them quickly.

1 **There is a sales- or product-led culture.** All too often marketing is viewed as the poor cousin to sales or product development. This sales- or product-led culture is particularly prevalent in technology-oriented sectors where there is a view that the company just needs to sell the latest, greatest, fastest, coolest products to a waiting public. If marketing is just about advertising, communications and PR, then this might be justified. But marketing is more than that – it should also be about understanding customers and markets and creating offerings to profitably meet their wants and needs.

2 **Marketing is a victim of short-term financial thinking.**
Because other functions such as finance and sales don't
understand marketing, they often just look at the available
numbers and take arbitrary, short-term decisions that act to
toggle marketing on and off, with a variety of serious ongoing
implications. If the revenue figures or sales pipeline are looking
weak then marketing will be expected to take short-term action
to bolster the numbers. This results in rushed, short-term promotions that might improve revenue but are at the expense of
margin and market positioning. If the numbers are worse and
cuts are in order then the marketing budget always seems to
be first in line for the axe. There are some valid reasons for
this. Marketing has an easily identified, discretionary budget
that seems to have few strings attached. But if marketing is
performing the role it should, then this approach is harmful to
the longer-term health of the business.

3 **Marketing is not viewed as a valued professional function.**
Here is another catch-22 – because marketing is too often
undervalued it does not attract enough capable, qualified and
energetic people to make a difference and challenge the
status quo. The reaction I got from my colleagues when I first
moved from sales to marketing was certainly not supportive! It
is good that people move into marketing with experience of
many other areas of the business, but more needs to be done
to elevate marketing from being a refuge for sales, clerical or
support staff looking for their next career move. And the marketing profession needs to raise its game to ensure greater
board representation.

4 **Marketing is too much art and not enough science.**
Marketing is in part a creative discipline, certainly with regard
to the communications side of the role. However, in order to
combat being seen as the 'coloured pen brigade', marketing
needs to balance creativity with a level of business acumen,
management science, analysis and strategic thinking. It is the
strength of these combined attributes that should make marketing the powerhouse of the business.

5 **It is difficult to demonstrate marketing's value.** Just as we feel other functions should better understand marketing, so marketing should have a greater awareness of other business roles, particularly finance. This is important in understanding how marketing is adding value to the business. Actual and measurable values must be understood and then communicated if the contribution of marketing is to be recognised. As a start, it should be mandatory for marketing managers to attend a 'finance for non-financial managers' programme.

 CASE STORY *HEWLETT PACKARD MARKETING BASICS,*
CLAIRE'S STORY

Narrator Claire was the marketing manager for one of Hewlett Packard's divisions in Europe.

Context With almost 50 years of innovation since being founded in the famous garage, by the early 1990s Hewlett Packard (HP) had expanded through its 50 or so divisions into a wide number of markets, including technical and commercial computing, test and measurement equipment, printing and imaging, and software. Although not known as a vocal marketing company, the business had very strong behind-the-scenes marketing processes – including in Claire's division.

Issue Known for engineering and service excellence, the business was extending both its markets and its products, talking to new customers and facing new competitors such as Sun and Apollo in key growth markets such as workstations. Divisions and sales groups needed to get closer to customers in order to sell existing products and develop successful new ones, rather than continuing to engineer 'better mousetraps'.

Solution Claire's division was involved in the extensive research and customer engagement programmes that were implemented across the company to understand fully what customers wanted from HP products and how they derived value from them. Through both external researchers and internal staff, HP tried to understand the customer value chain and how customers went about their business using HP products to deliver value. As well as working directly with customers, Claire's division engaged with partners to learn from their understanding of the market and capture a true 360-degree view.

> **Learning** This was an era when many businesses transitioned from being product- and sales-centric to customer-centric, where the customer was always right. HP took the better path of becoming market-centric, amalgamating customer feedback into addressable market opportunities. The business then started the process of balancing the innovative, engineering heritage with the new-found market focus and was able to grow from strength to strength.

6 **Marketing becomes a support function.** If marketing is viewed simply as a sales support function, it will forever be doomed to fail. In that situation strong sales numbers are the result of the successful, capable and well-led sales team, while poor numbers result from ineffective or insufficient marketing support and lead generation. This is closely related to the 'sell what we've got' mentality. Instead, marketing and sales should be highly aligned and integrated, with a single view of the customer and the pipeline. Then marketing is responsible for the management and regulation of the sales pipeline while sales focuses on closing qualified opportunities.

7 **Short-term pressures take focus away from the value drivers.** Of course it's important to deliver the numbers on a monthly or quarterly basis, but equally it's critical that businesses don't lose sight of the longer-term role of marketing. I'm not even talking here of the management of product life cycles. From communication and promotion through to customers that can be referenced, marketing should be managing a single, closed-loop demand generation process that provides feedback at all stages. Managing the process is then about optimising the flow and feedback as efficiently as possible, from an unaware but addressable market at one end to satisfied, reference customers at the other. A bit like peristalsis in the human digestive tract. Short-term activities should only be taken with a system perspective, to restore balance or increase the flow through the entire system. They should not be knee-jerk actions that simply focus on one stage and so disrupt the balance, reduce margins and potentially damage the brand.

8 **There is a lack of professional development.** Despite the efforts of the Chartered Institute of Marketing and business schools around the country, marketing still suffers from a lack of professional development. The fact that staff are recruited from a variety of roles has a significant impact on a team's ability to operate at the highest levels, and too much skills development is left to chance or done on the hop.

9 **Senior management pays lip service to marketing.** Is this because marketing is viewed as part of sales rather than the other way around? Perhaps senior management simply views marketing as a necessary cost rather than as a strategic enabler of the business. Some might argue that marketing should be less of an isolated function and more the responsibility of everyone in the business, supported by a small guiding team. Therefore senior board-level market representation isn't needed. But the same could be argued for much of the HR role, so why is HR represented on every board and marketing on so few?

10 **Marketing is not managed as a consistent, repeatable process.** Related to the lack of management science, the creative nature of marketing sometimes becomes an excuse for poor levels of control, predictability and repeatability. This does no favours for the marketing team's credibility with the board. For the most part, finance, sales, production, operations and other business functions are now based around data-driven, repeatable processes, and so marketing, too, needs to step up to the mark if it is to earn the respect it warrants.

So just what is marketing? – frequently asked questions

The following table provides quick answers to some of the most frequently asked questions about marketing. Use this as a way of gaining a quick overview on the key issues and challenges.

FAQ 1 *What is marketing?*	**1** The business process by which organisations identify, create, communicate and deliver offerings and solutions to meet customer wants and needs that they either know and recognise now or will do in the near future. This process delivers experiences for target markets and builds reputations for brands and the organisation.
FAQ 2 *How should we identify market opportunities?*	**2** The two most common approaches are to deliver new products to existing markets and customers, or to seek new markets for the current range. The key for either is to gain a fundamental understanding of customer behaviours and how your offering impacts them and is valued. As with many things, it is more perspiration than inspiration, so do your primary and secondary research, talk to customers, analyse the results and regularly brainstorm opportunities as a team.
FAQ 3 *Do we really need a marketing department?*	**3** Not necessarily, but there needs to be top-level commitment and a focused resource of some kind to drive the development of the business and deliver the strategic role of marketing as described above. As long as that happens, it is feasible to distribute or even outsource many of the remaining aspects of the marketing delivery. Without a formal marketing department, many more people across the business need to embrace and practise the basic principles of marketing.
FAQ 4 *How much should we spend on marketing?*	**4** That really depends on the type of business you're in. In general terms you should be thinking of a minimum of 5 per cent of revenues, but that could rise to over 25 per cent. Think about the large budgets that Red Bull or Nike or Dell spend on marketing. They certainly create an impact for the money. Marketing is the second biggest cost item for a pharmaceutical company, behind R&D. But nobody knows what the average spend is, and to a large extent it's totally irrelevant. The only thing that really matters is what your objectives are and how much it will cost to achieve them. It will make a huge difference depending on whether you are offering a commodity or a differentiated solution. In short, there is no right answer. Try to benchmark against competitors and closely monitor spend against returns and business results.

FAQ 5 *Does the internet make marketing redundant?*	5 Far from it. The internet is another tool/ technology that can be used or misused just as any other, and so it simply it adds another dimension to marketing. You don't have to be selling online to benefit from the market reach that the internet can provide. It has catalysed some basic changes in economic behaviour and you should explore its power to impact marketing and customer behaviour. Use it wisely and effectively and it could transform the business. Ignore it at your peril: in the internet age reputations can be damaged very quickly.
FAQ 6 *Why is marketing important when the business is strong?*	6 It's a bit like asking why Roger Federer and Tiger Woods bother practising when they are already quite good. Continual improvement aims to build on strengths and eliminate weaknesses, so since marketing in its fullest sense has probably the greatest ability to impact the ongoing success of the business it would seem to be a wise investment of time and resource. If you stand still, everyone else will catch up.
FAQ 7 *Why is marketing also important when revenues, profits and costs are under pressure?*	7 If we believe marketing is the engine of strategic business development, then marketing must play a major role when times are tough. When competitive pressures increase, through industry change or economic downturn, most businesses need to search for opportunities to increase their differentiation rather than cut back. Yes, the pressure is on to contain costs, so marketing needs to ensure it's being efficient and effective, innovative and well managed, but the only way out is to strengthen marketing and the proposition so that customers are more inclined to buy your offering at sustainable margins. And the tougher the conditions, the more important this is.
FAQ 8 *Who should marketing include and involve in the strategic process?*	8 The temptation is to say 'As many people as possible', but that can obviously get out of hand and would not help in building consensus. So let's narrow it down to senior management or their appointed delegates from finance, sales and production or operations. There are always exceptions to this short list, but it's a good start. Obviously the executive team needs to understand and buy into the marketing strategy, but at least active input and involvement from senior members of these key functional areas should help to ensure that the business is aligned.

FAQ 9 *Is marketing a creative art or a management science?*	**9** A bit of both, but the point is that sometimes the emphasis has been too much on the creative elements rather than the management science. Guinness is famed for its award-winning creative advertising. These ads are certainly noticed and talked about by the general public, but it's only through rigorous and integrated management that the ads translate into sustained sales of the black stuff. The point is that the creative side is only really a means to an end – and so (to stretch the use of catchphrases) should not be allowed to wag the management dog!
FAQ 10 *How should I measure marketing performance?*	**10** Because of the multifaceted nature of marketing, it is essential to capture a range of performance indicators in a scorecard or dashboard. The actual key performance indicators (KPIs) will be selected depending on your business drivers, but could include, for example: elements of market share performance; revenue mix by channel or product or new versus repeat business; brand recognition or equity; and customer behaviour or response. Don't get lulled into measuring the easy numbers or the lagging indicators just because they are accessible, as those aren't necessarily the ones that show current performance or direction.
FAQ 11 *How should we track return on marketing investment?*	**11** Ideally you should track return on marketing investment (ROMI) on multiple levels to establish measures of effectiveness and efficiency. As a minimum you should look to measure this by programme/campaign. First of all, you need to ensure that the numbers and metrics are financially sound, otherwise they will be meaningless to the people reading them. Input investment figures are easy, as they are just what you have spent. The two critical elements are to get agreement on the value of a given performance indicator and, if there's any doubt, on the correlation between it and the marketing input that drives it. Keep it simple to start with, but consider moving to more complete approaches using net present values, particularly for long-term programmes. When using ROMI for planning purposes, you should also look at opportunity costs when selecting approaches in a resource-constrained environment.

FAQ 12 *Is marketing just for businesses selling to consumers rather than other businesses?*

12 Not at all. While consumer markets traditionally represent the largest and most visible marketing sector, the fastest growth area in recent years has been business-to-business (B2B) marketing, with areas such as channel marketing. Industrial or B2B markets are often more complex than consumer ones and require specific skills and a combination of both broad and deep market understanding. One big difference is that B2B markets are more needs- or solution-based, with customers dissecting value propositions, as opposed to many 'want'- and emotion-based consumer markets.

FAQ 13 *What is the best way to keep marketing activities aligned and on track?*

13 Professional marketing teams should be using support tools to help manage the marketing life cycle and ensure that activities are integrated and aligned with strategies and business goals. By incorporating project and programme management techniques, such tools help to keep track of timescales, budgets, activity and the resulting impact. By providing management reports they should broadly eliminate the time-wasting tedium of manual monthly reporting, as all the information is already in the system. They should also help marketing decision making, and support running a self-sustaining, closed-loop marketing function that understands, plans, executes and reviews its markets, strategies and activities.

FAQ 14 *Should I split team resources by function or market?*

14 Ideally you would have the resources to have a combination of both, but often this is not the case. Roles such as PR and product marketing do tend to be function-specific, with a broad remit across the whole business. By definition, product marketing tends to address not just the products but also the markets to which those products are sold. However, it is often important to have specific expertise in key vertical or even horizontal markets in order to communicate in relevant and meaningful ways with target customers.

FAQ 15 How should we handle competitors moving the goal posts?

15 There are a myriad of ways. This is as much a fundamental business strategy as marketing. How does the business want to compete? What are the dynamics of the markets you operate in? A market-follower strategy or certain markets might dictate that you drop prices in response to a competitor, but unless you drive cost savings then all that happens is that you make less margin. Some competitive actions drive increased margins. Starbucks has enabled a whole industry to sell coffee variants at almost ten times the price of petrol! So whether you go in the opposite direction, stop playing their game and start your own, follow them or ignore them, it's a great opportunity to test the market and perhaps rethink your strategic approach.

FAQ 16 What about marketing internally?

16 This is a very important and sometimes underrated area. Many businesses view employees as a key asset, but too often forget to take them on the journey. Internal marketing should be working on a number of levels. Don't just tell employees about the vision and what the business stands for. Marketing should be delivering customer messages internally as well, to make sure everyone is on the same page. This is not just effective 'soft' management but critical in aligning the business around customers and markets. All too often there are examples of finance sending out threatening letters at the same time as marketing is encouraging the same customers to spend more money.

FAQ 17 What factors dictate a direct or indirect route to market?

17 The decision to market and sell directly or indirectly through distribution channels is partly dictated by overall business strategy, but key factors include the relationship between the addressable market and your resources to access it, the time you have to establish your market presence in it and your knowledge of and access to customers in it. Whether you are looking at a multi-tier distribution model, with retailers or resellers eventually selling to end customers, or a franchise model to rapidly establish a brand, the choice will come down to leverage and market access versus the cost and/or risk.

FAQ 18 *Should we have one big brand or several sub-brands?*	**18** There is no right or wrong answer to this. Often there will be historic reasons for any given situation. One can argue that simplification and clarity are good and that resources should be focused on the overall brand. Alternatively, different brands might be needed to appeal to different markets and customers. Think of car makers such as Toyota, Lexus or VW and all their brands, including Bugatti, Lamborghini, Audi, Skoda and Seat. Sub-brands are often product groupings that can be positioned and priced more easily for target segments, as demonstrated by the Oakley sunglasses range, Canon's EOS digital SLR cameras, or Nikon's COOLPIX consumer range.
FAQ 19 *Should marketing be involved with acquisitions?*	**19** As both are related and both are key strategic drivers for the business, the answer should be 'yes'. Dedicated acquisitions and corporate development teams are often slightly secretive, removed and perhaps self-contained, for obvious confidentiality reasons. But they don't always have strategic marketing backgrounds. Senior, strategic marketing people should be the ones initially identifying the market opportunities for the business that then require broader input on the make-or-buy decision. This is not something for the whole marketing team, but appropriate people should be involved from this stage right through to integration planning.
FAQ 20 *How does marketing relate to innovation?*	**20** The answer has to be 'very closely'. Innovation applies across the whole business, but much innovation is focused around products and markets and so impacts marketing significantly. If innovation has any strategic input, it must stem from the market opportunity and make-or-buy decisions that provide medium-term direction for the business. Marketing and innovation also relate at the tactical level – for example, where a product innovation enables a premium price or a clear differentiation in a dynamic market, such as the SanDisk SD+ memory card that also fits directly into a USB socket.

I hope that these FAQs give a quick start to getting to grips with marketing. The rest of this book shows you how to move from understanding what the key elements of marketing are to an active implementation of marketing techniques, either within your team or division or across the company.

EXPERT VOICE

Positioning marketing in the innovation process

Professor Jean-Jacques Chanaron

As firms prepare for the new world after recession, there is little doubt that the emphasis will shift from cost containment and the short term to business building and the long term. Knowing when to shift the focus is a judgement call that many senior executives leave too late. But it is extremely difficult to persuade companies to invest in the future when the future is seen as being only short term and about survival. Business building is an area where the marketing function has a key role to play and often this implies innovation. To play this role, however, those in marketing need to understand the nature of firm innovation and how it is changing.

Since the 1970s, the economics and management of innovation have raised considerable attention from scholars worldwide at theoretical, practical and clinical levels. This is mainly due to the assumption that the number and pace of innovations have increased significantly during this period, contributing to the rise of the so-called knowledge society. Innovation is now placed at the very front end of corporate strategy and culture.

Key academic contributions emphasise the shift from a vision of a process of innovation as a series of sequential stages from fundamental research to commercial success for isolated events or artefacts, to a vision of a systemic social process of interaction between the various stakeholders. The end requirement is that the innovative idea is scientifically and technically possible, industrially feasible, socially acceptable and economically viable.

Scholars agree that the 'saltationistic' approach of regular technological revolution, generating a cluster of new products, new services, new processes and new markets, is probably not any more valid and that a 'gradualistic' evolutionary approach is more realistic.

Scholars emphasise that the key success factor for technological as well as organisational innovations is a large consensus amongst stakeholders that such innovative products, services, processes or business models have a significant tangible socio-economic added value (see figure on the next page). They also pinpoint that innovativeness comes from a full alignment of innovation strategy with the overall corporate strategic intent, an appropriate climate and culture for newness and change, and an early involvement of customers and users during the process.

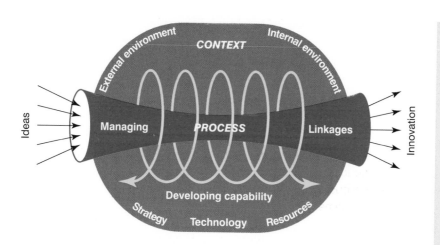

Researchers have also reported that an excess of formalisation of such innovation processes within organisations, in particular small to medium-sized enterprises, has a negative impact on creativity and therefore on innovativeness. It is recommended that organisations should prioritise the creation of an empowering culture, through high responsiveness to individuals, being supportive of their innovation efforts and placing value on those individuals who are involved in the innovation process, including through specific reward systems. It is also highly recommended that companies put in place agile and adaptative organisations and procedures for managing the innovation process, allowing measurement and benchmarking.

Two of the ongoing topics at the top of the agenda in economic and management research about innovation deal with disruptive innovation and open innovation systems. Anticipating and managing radical innovations that might provide substantial competitive advantage is obviously a crucial challenge, due to the high level of uncertainty and risk. So far, there is no theoretical model and scholars are looking for lessons from best practices.

The open innovation philosophy states that innovative ideas are widely distributed, that innovating is a process of poker as well as chess, and that ideas should be taken from everywhere and not only from internal research and development capabilities: research units, suppliers and customers, as well as competitors. Creating, developing and running efficiently innovation-oriented networks is becoming a key strategic corporate competence and managing intellectual property is now a key strategic issue. It is then recommended that organisations give priority to being outwardly focused, indicating a systematic attempt to understand features of the changing marketplace and general business environment and sharing that understanding across the whole organisation.

One of the key challenges facing marketers is recognising their skills and potential contribution to the processes of creating new business and then ensuring that these are well used in moving the organisation forward, as well as in building their own personal careers.

MARKETING AUDIT

To improve performance, you first need to understand where you are starting from. What are your strengths and weaknesses and how will each promote or limit your ability to achieve? There are two levels of awareness you need to have. The first is to understand what the most successful marketing teams or businesses look like, how they behave and how near your team is to emulating them. The second is to understand what it takes to lead such a team – do you personally have the necessary attributes for success?

Team assessment

Is my marketing team maximising its potential?

Use the following checklist[1] to assess the current state of your team and organisation with regard to all the elements of the marketing function. Consider each element in turn and use a simple Red-Amber-Green evaluation. Red reflects areas where you disagree strongly with the statement and suggests there are significant issues requiring immediate attention, and Amber suggests areas of concern and risk. Green means that you are happy with the current state.

---

[1] Integrated Marketing Framework, Sine Qua Non International Ltd, 2008.

ID	CATEGORY	EVALUATION CRITERIA	STATUS
Marketing			RAG
M1	Principles: marketing basics	Marketing is recognised as a strategic priority: it is owned by a member of the senior executive team and is aligned and focused on meeting the needs of clearly defined markets of accessible customers with a clear and succinct unique selling proposition (USP)	☐
M2	Process: understand	The marketing team is sufficiently skilled and allocates enough time and resources to fully understanding behaviours, trends, dynamics and data about active and adjacent markets	☐
M3	Process: develop	Marketing activities are developed in an active, structured manner to address opportunities and threats through a consistent and targeted strategic process	☐
M4	Process: execute	The team has the project and programme management skills to consistently implement marketing plans, delivering against goals and objectives efficiently, on time and within budget	☐
M5	Process: review	Marketing plans and activities are closed-loop and the team completes each programme with a learning and review cycle to evaluate results, insights and potential improvement opportunities	☐
M6	Portfolio management	Marketing elements, including activities, products and brands, are managed actively as dynamic portfolios with interplays thought through	☐
M7	Positioning: inside-out thinking and positioning	Products and services are defined in terms of the four Ps of product, price, promotion and place, to ensure that well-defined products are delivered profitably and competitively through appropriate channels to target markets	☐
M8	Positioning: outside-in thinking and positioning	Market offerings are considered, positioned and communicated in terms of the four Rs of relevance, receptivity, responsiveness and relationship, to ensure that audiences are engaged meaningfully	☐
M9	Programme choices	The team is skilled at employing a full range and mix of marketing programme types to engage with key audiences effectively	☐
M10	Performance management	Key performance indicators, scorecards and objectives for marketing exist to provide a visible performance management framework from which to judge success and opportunities for improvement	☐

Complete the checklist and quickly map out the capabilities and practices so that you can see how the team stacks up. Having identified where the gaps are in your business or team capabilities, you need to understand if you are the right person to be leading the marketing team.

Self-assessment

Do I have what it takes?

This section presents a self-assessment checklist of the factors that make a successful Fast Track marketing leader. These reflect the knowledge, competencies, attitudes and behaviours required to get to the top, irrespective of your current level of seniority. Take control of your career, behave professionally and reflect on your personal vision for the next five years. This creates a framework for action throughout the rest of the book.

Use the checklist overleaf to identify where you personally need to gain knowledge or skills. Fill it in honestly and then get someone who knows you well – your boss or a key member of your team – to go over it with you. Be willing to change your assessment if people give you insights into yourself that you had not taken into account.

Use the following scoring process:

0 A totally new area of knowledge or skills

1 You are aware of the area but have low knowledge and lack skills

2 An area where you are reasonably competent and working on improvement

3 An area where you have a satisfactory level of knowledge and skills

4 An area where you are consistently well above average

5 You are recognised as a key figure in this area of knowledge and skills throughout the business

Reflect on the lowest scores and identify those areas that are critical to success. Flag these as status Red, requiring immediate attention. Then identify those areas that you are concerned about and flag those as status Amber, implying areas of development that need to be monitored closely.

ID	CATEGORY	EVALUATION CRITERIA	SCORE	STATUS
	Knowledge		0–5	RAG
K1	Industry and markets	Knowledge of your industry in terms of overall size and growth, key players, competitive forces and major trends. This should also include an understanding of the broad segmentation of products and markets	☐	☐
K2	Customers and competitors	Information and understanding about major customers, in terms of who they are, their must-haves, wants and needs and their drivers. An understanding of who the best competitors are, what they do and how they perform	☐	☐
K3	Products and services	An understanding of current products and/or services and how they stack up in the marketplace against the industry leaders. This should include substitutes or solutions available from companies in different industries	☐	☐
K4	Tools and techniques	Insights into current and emerging marketing tools and techniques that will impact on how you access and communicate with audiences in your market	☐	☐
	Competencies			
C1	Creative thinking	Ability to think out of the box and use various techniques to challenge the current state. Ability to identify new product, market, messaging or process improvement breakthroughs	☐	☐
C2	Problem solving	Ability to break down problems and think through issues logically, appraising a situation and analysing factors to find solutions and enable performance breakthroughs	☐	☐
C3	Project management	Ability to define, plan, monitor and control activities in order to deliver identified programmes and initiatives on time and within budget		
C4	Risk management	Ability to think ahead and identify, prioritise and mitigate issues and barriers to effective implementation	☐	☐

ID	CATEGORY	EVALUATION CRITERIA	SCORE	STATUS
Attitudes			0–5	RAG
A1	Positive outlook	More than looking on the bright side, this is the belief that you can make things happen and make a difference. It is not being a victim of circumstance even if it means facing some resistance from other people or events	☐	☐
A2	Search for synergies	Willingness to look for synergies in terms of ideas or capabilities, whether among the team or with external resources. Ability to combine creatively the best of these to develop new and exciting concepts	☐	☐
A3	Enquiring mindset	Willingness to question convention and ask why things are as they are. Ability to think through the reasons from different angles while constantly seeking more effective or efficient ways of doing things	☐	☐
A4	Breakthrough thinking	Not getting stuck in incremental thinking and improvement. Looking for ways to upset the apple cart and redefine approaches or markets to dramatically change the way the business operates	☐	☐
Behaviours				
B1	Determination and commitment	Willingness to see things through, despite setbacks. Leading from the front and showing that you're going to do what it takes to make it happen	☐	☐
B2	Open and active	Welcoming open approaches and ideas from people but demonstrating support for priority ideas in the way you allocate your time, resources and budgets	☐	☐
B3	Encouragement	Always enthusiastic in coaching and mentoring others in the team. Always looking for ways in which you can be a catalyst for improvement in the team, encouraging them to develop and grow	☐	☐
B4	Positive challenge	Challenging the status quo and the ideas of others in a positive way, helping people to think things through from different perspectives	☐	☐

CASE STORY *TECHNOLOGY RESELLER, ANNABEL'S STORY*

Narrator Annabel is the marketing executive responsible for all marketing activity in five key target sectors for the company.

Context The business sells both IT and data and voice networking solutions to a wide range of customers in terms of size, location and vertical industry. During a period of rapid growth, the company had expanded its salesforce but added few resources to marketing. This was because marketing was often viewed as unnecessary and expensive when business was flowing in through the door anyway.

Issue The sales department was very much in control so it was often difficult to get support when Annabel looked at opportunities for marketing initiatives, particularly promotions. Although Annabel reported to the sales director, it became clear that marketing effort was being wasted by a salesforce who just went their own way. A typical example was the resistance of salespeople when asked to follow up a mailshot with the necessary telephone canvassing.

Solution Annabel got the agreement of the sales director to present a case to the managing director that he should change his title to 'sales and marketing director'. This simple change made the salespeople pay more attention to the initiatives that marketing was promoting and gained their invaluable input as to what should be done.

Learning Any staff job that isn't directly generating sales in a smaller company – but particularly a marketing role – needs a top-level sponsor to ensure that the line managers take it seriously. Given that the sales team are key internal customers but also resources for the marketing team (although sales would never agree with this point!), it is essential to get sales and marketing in alignment and working together for the good of the business.

Audit summary

Take a few minutes to reflect on the leadership–team effectiveness matrix opposite and consider your current position: where are you and what are the implications?

→ **Bottom left – poor leadership and an ineffective team.** This will result in failure – who knows, you may already be too late.

→ **Top left – great leadership but a poor team.** You have a great vision but you will be unlikely to implement it and so it will have little impact. You will need to find a way of taking people with you, and introducing systems and processes to improve team effectiveness.

→ **Bottom right – poor leadership but a great team.** You are highly effective and efficient as a team but may well be going in the wrong direction. It is no use being the most innovative and efficient developers of black and white televisions if there is no market!

→ **Top right – clear leadership and direction combined with an efficient and effective team.** This is where we want to be. Lots of great new ideas for marketing linked to current business goals and with a team unit capable of delivering on time and within budget. You don't need this book – please give it to someone else!

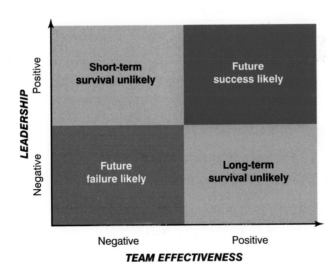

STOP – THINK – ACT

Part A has given you a quick overview of what marketing is, and you will also have assessed the performance of yourself and your team against best practice checklists. This will have raised your awareness of what is possible and clarified where you are now.

At the end of the individual and team audits take time to reflect on your profile in order to:

1 identify any 'quick wins' you could achieve today;
2 use the rest of the book effectively.

Look for areas where you could get a 'quick win' and improve matters in the short term. Ask yourself and the team these questions:

What should we do?	What will we change today and what difference will it make (why)? How will we know if it has been successful?
Who do we need to involve?	Who else needs to be involved to make it work and why?
What resources will we require?	What information, facilities, materials, equipment or budget will be required and are they available?
What is the timing?	When will this change be implemented – is there a deadline?

Visit **www.Fast-Track-Me.com** to use the Fast Track online planning tool.

Service-dominant logic

Professor Caroline Tynan

EXPERT VOICE

Marketing is in trouble. Its influence on senior management is decreasing as fewer marketing directors have a seat on the board, and as those board positions are increasingly short-lived. Marketing is no longer seen as the function that understands the customer, and astonishingly, a recent study from the USA indicated that only 10 per cent of board time was spent on marketing and customer-related issues. This decline can be linked to the gap between the traditional marketing ideas we teach and the world that marketing practitioners see on a daily basis.

The response of marketing academics to this crisis has emerged in some new thinking known as service-dominant logic (S-D logic). Its authors, Steve Vargo and Robert Lusch,[2] positioned their work as the first 'open source' marketing theory, and by doing that they have stimulated an unprecedented amount of debate, discussion and development of their initial ideas as the rest of the academic world 'pimp their model'.

So how do the ideas of S-D logic differ from the traditional marketing mix ones that were taught in the past?

This new market-grounded view of value and exchange changes the key focus of marketing from creating value through physical goods that are then delivered to the customer, to a focus on co-creating **value with customers** through the application of knowledge, skills, processes and competences. So, with S-D logic thinking, marketing is about **experiences** delivered through service, and not about goods and products.

These ideas bring with them a number of significant implications for marketers, including the need to concentrate on co-creating **value in use** – that is, value enjoyed when the customer uses the offering, rather than simply considering the value at the point of exchange. Customers co-create value from many sources in addition to the functional features of a product (including sensory, emotional, cognitive, relational, behavioural, informational and social ones) before, during and after the consumption experience, so these potential sources of value should all be taken into account in the co-creation process.

There are many players involved in the **network** that co-creates value for the customer, including fellow customers, external experts and opinion leaders, brand communities and stakeholders. Co-creation is achieved by jointly and flexibly **interacting** with customers and network members and engaging them in **dialogue**. The interaction involves sharing sensitive information and engaging in joint problem solving, and so requires high levels of trust, indicating that marketers must give evidence of being trustworthy by being honest, reliable and open in their dealings with, and demonstrating commitment to, the customer throughout. The success of these processes also requires organisational learning to capitalise on the knowledge gained.

Our current understandings of marketing need to be considerably revised to incorporate the ideas of S-D logic. It advocates a focus on service rather than goods or services, the co-creation of experiences, the necessity of engaging in dialogue with customers, the offering of a total value proposition, the participation in a value-creation network, flexibility and rapid adaptation, and learning to offer solutions achieved by jointly working with

[2] Vargo, S.L. and Lusch, R.F. (2004), 'Evolving to a new dominant logic for marketing', *Journal of Marketing*, 68, 1–17.

EXPERT VOICE

customers. Implementing these new ideas suggests a long-term strategy that encompasses a shared vision delivering mutually negotiated experiences through collaboration as partners in an extensive network.

Although these new ideas may be difficult to implement, they offer the promise of a revival for marketing and a profitable way forward. 〞

PART B

BUSINESS
FAST TRACK

rrespective of your chosen function or discipline, look around at the successful managers whom you know and admire. We call these people Fast Track managers, people who have the knowledge and skills to perform well and fast track their careers. Notice how they excel at three things:

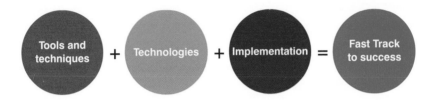

Tools and techniques
They have a good understanding of best practices for their particular field. This is in the form of methods and techniques that translate knowledge into decisions, insights and actions. They understand what the best companies do and have an ability to interpret what is relevant for their own businesses. The processes they use are generally simple to explain and form a logical step-by-step approach to solving a problem or capturing data and insights. They also encourage creativity – Fast Track managers do not follow a process slavishly where they know they are filling in the boxes rather than looking for insights on how to improve performance. This combination of method and creativity produces the optimum solutions.

They also have a clear understanding of what is important to know and what is simply noise. They either know this information or have it at their fingertips as and when they require it. They also have effective filtering mechanisms so that they don't get overloaded with extraneous information. The level of detail required varies dramatically from one situation to another – the small entrepreneur will work a lot more on the knowledge they have and in gaining facts from quick conversations with experts, whereas a large corporate may employ teams of analysts and research companies. Frequently when a team is going through any process they uncover the need for further data.

Technologies

However, having the facts and understanding best practice will achieve little unless they are built into the systems that people use on a day-to-day basis. Fast Track managers use appropriate technologies to maximise both effectiveness and efficiency.

Implementation

Finally, having designed the framework that is appropriate to them and their team, Fast Track managers are also great at implementation, putting in place the changes necessary to build and sustain the performance of the team.

The next chapters will outline the structures and processes that cover all these topics, but the choice as to how tightly or loosely you will use them will vary, and will to a certain extent depend on personal style. As you read through the following three chapters, first seek to understand how each idea could impact you and your team, and then decide what level of implementation may be appropriate given your starting point, authority and aspirations.

FAST TRACK TOP TEN

This chapter presents a framework of methods or techniques to improve performance and make life as part of a marketing team easier. Each element can take a lifetime to master, but the Fast Track manager will know which areas to focus on – get those areas right and the team will perform. Often success relates to the introduction of simple tools and techniques to improve effectiveness and efficiency.

Introducing marketing tools and techniques

What needs to be included? – the top ten tools and techniques

You will have probably heard of the four Ps of marketing – product, price, promotion and placement – and we shall be exploring them further later on. In fact the top ten tools and techniques for the Fast Track marketing team are captured within an integrated framework of six Ps.

Principles set out the overall goals and challenges of marketing in today's business environment. By reminding ourselves of the fundamental principles of marketing, we stand a better chance of achieving the ends – the business objectives – rather than getting caught up in the means by which they are achieved:

1 Marketing basics (the foundations and essential elements of strategic and operational marketing)

Process addresses the four phases of strategic marketing management and delivery that ensure marketing activity is a continuous, sustainable cycle. This approach applies the 'systems thinking' of the Toyota production system or the Honda plan-do-check-act cycle to the marketing environment:

2 Understand (all factors, external and internal, impacting on the situation)

3 Develop (strategies and plans to address opportunities and deliver objectives)

4 Execute (and deliver activities to realise those plans)

5 Review (the learning phase, evaluating and feeding back results and insights gleaned from the process)

Portfolios include the brands, products, audiences and activities that marketing teams must direct to achieve their goals. Portfolios and their management are critical to marketing success because thinking in terms of portfolios ensures that all aspects of your marketing effort are integrated and consistent. Portfolio management gives you the overall control of all the activities that are managed by or contributed to by the marketing department:

6 Portfolio management (building, nurturing, pruning, balancing and orchestrating)

Positioning is one of the key disciplines at the heart of marketing. The much maligned but often used SWOT (strengths, weaknesses, opportunities and threats) analysis looks at strengths and weaknesses from an internal perspective and opportunities and threats externally. We will take a similar 360-degree perspective on positioning and supplement the predominantly inside-out thinking of the traditional four Ps with the outside-in market or recipient perspective of the four Rs:

7 Inside-out thinking and positioning – the four Ps (product, price, placement and promotion)

8 Outside-in thinking and positioning – the four Rs (relevance, receptivity, responsiveness and relationship)

Programmes are the most visible output from the marketing activity. This element explores some of the programme options available to address the positioning challenges and suggests some potential winning approaches:

9 Programme choices (tools and options)

Performance completes the cycle by evaluating how the marketing function has performed against the business objectives:

10 Performance management (evaluation, metrics and returns)

These six Ps are not a sequential tick-list for marketing management excellence, but instead offer a view of the marketing challenge from a number of different perspectives. Combining these approaches and applying them to your own environment should cover all the basics.

 CASE STORY SANDISK, TANYA'S STORY

Narrator Tanya was the director responsible for product marketing across the memory card business.

Context SanDisk is the leader in the flash memory market, delivering products that include Sansa music and video players, high performance photographic memory cards in a variety of formats, mobile phone memory cards, USB memory products and a range of card readers. SanDisk holds many flash memory patents and licenses products to other manufacturers, as well as selling to consumers through retailers throughout the world.

Issue The flash memory market has many low-cost producers which, combined with a rapidly declining price per megabyte as a result of technology advances and market forces, tends to commoditise the market. SanDisk was and still is the market share leader with the popular range of 'Ultra' photographic cards for the consumer market. So the issue facing Tanya was how to combat those market forces.

Solution The answer lay in understanding the market trends and dynamics and developing a parallel brand to meet the needs of advanced and professional users. Tanya proposed and developed the new 'Extreme' photo cards that are now the recognised best-of-class product for these high-end users. With this one move, she addressed an untapped market opportunity while also delivering a 'halo' product line that reinforces and supports SanDisk's leadership position in the broader market. Tanya

> marketed the 'Extreme' line as the preferred choice of the serious photographer and integrated it into SanDisk's Ducati sponsorship, thus making the SanDisk brand more visible overall.
>
> **Learning** The success of the 'Extreme' cards demonstrated how a solid understanding of markets and some clear thinking can turn a potential threat into an opportunity to develop your market position. In one move SanDisk created a high-end leadership product and an effective response to increasing commoditisation.

1 PRINCIPLES Marketing basics

As obvious as it may seem, a recap of the principles of marketing is vital to keeping marketing on the Fast Track to success. The very first step is to agree on what marketing is there to do for the business. Too many people focus on just one aspect of marketing, such as advertising, and take that to be the role of marketing. Others confuse marketing with sales or product management. The former can often lead to short-term, revenue-chasing activity that delivers no enduring gains in terms of marketing goals. Worse, it can even damage brands or margins. The widespread move away from emphasising customer satisfaction and towards emphasising customer experience is now a major factor in marketing, but again is only one part of the picture.

Marketing is about matching the competencies and capabilities of businesses with the wants and needs of customers. It sounds simple but there are a lot of variables in there, and that is probably where much of the confusion arises. Marketing is not just about advertising to find some customers to buy the products that we make. Equally, it's not just about researching customers to find out about wants and needs so that we can deliver appropriate products or services. It is a constant, interactive balancing act, communicating and configuring propositions to and fro between target customers and the company. You should approach all interactions with customers, prospects or other market stakeholders as opportunities to input to this equation, checking responses to propositions and market requirements.

Given that in most circumstances we are not operating with a clean sheet but instead with legacy propositions, the first stake in the ground is probably a product or service offering. So the first task is to define the target audience for the proposition. This process of segmentation is probably the hardest single task we face, for two reasons. The first is the sheer complexity, in terms of the number of variables and permutations of target customer wants and needs. The second is the understandable response of trying to appeal to as wide an audience as possible. This leads companies, for example, to define segments such as 'SMEs of less than 100 employees' as their targets, as though the thousands of such businesses in the UK had uniform wants and needs. Similarly, 'families with two pre-teenage children' are clearly such a divergent and varied consumer target that they represent a meaningless segment. The trick is to make the segment actionable, in terms of either your inputs or the responses of the target audience.

QUICK TIP *REVIEW THE BASICS*

To make sure you don't lose sight of the basics, check every so often that your proposition is still valid. What are you offering to which target customers and what differentiates you from the rest? Why is the proposition of interest or relevant to those targets and what value does it offer?

One other basic principle is the contrast between strategic and operational marketing. Marketing is and should be a strategic driver for the business. The matching activity described above (between the business and the customers) and the inherent targeting required are part management science and process, part analytical assessment and only part the creative input so often associated with marketing. As such, the marketing function should be managed as a strategic process rather than as a loose, creative activity. It should be closely aligned with the business goals, and as a result closely allied to the actual capability of the company and the experience delivered to the customer. **Strategic marketing** defines how the business aims to compete. An excellent example of this in the UK is John Lewis. The company has aligned its capabilities (first-class

buying of quality goods at keen prices, for example), its culture (very customer oriented with unusually knowledgeable staff) and its processes to
deliver a consistent experience that matches with the marketing promise.

Operational marketing is more about delivering programmes and
activities to make the strategic vision a reality. Resources, activity, programmes and offerings all need to be targeted accurately and directed
to ensure effective and efficient delivery of marketing objectives.
Evaluation and insights should be captured as part of the management
process and fed back into future activity.

Ideally, formalised tools and systems should be established to make
sure that marketing is managed in line with business goals and that
strategic and operational elements are in synch. Note that there is nothing to say that strategic marketing should not be pragmatic or that
operational marketing should not be approached strategically.

To summarise, strategic thinking is about long range vision – say a two-
to five-year horizon. That strategic thinking is driven by market data and
breakthrough innovation. An example would be the understanding of customers and technologies and the thinking behind the entry into a new
market arena such as location-based telephony services. Operational
thinking, on the other hand, is driven by the day-to-day needs of the business itself, such as building a revenue pipeline, and rarely looks beyond
the next 12 months.

The Fast Track marketing manager will never lose sight of these basic
marketing principles despite the myriad day-to-day distractions and
challenges of the marketing environment.

2 PROCESS _Understand_

The first step in the iterative, four-stage management process is that of
understanding. While Fast Track managers need to be action- and results-
oriented, this is best achieved by the 'ready, aim, fire' school of
management thinking rather than a quick-draw, short-term, knee-jerk
mentality. Only by understanding the internal drivers, the surrounding environment and the factors impacting on them at every level of activity can

the marketing manager deliver consistent results. This applies whether you are starting a longer-term strategic plan or a fast-impact tactical promotion, as the latter is just a lower-level iteration of the same process.

For example, consider the dynamic nature of the colour television market and its recent transition from old cathode ray tubes (CRT) to liquid crystal displays (LCD) and plasma screens. If you were a market player in either the old market or the new markets, it would have been essential to have a clear understanding of the factors driving customer behaviours, the erosion of the CRT market and the rapid uptake of flat screen technologies. These were driven by a combination of technology advances and scale economies to drive reduced prices, the switch to digital TV and high consumer spending as a result of affluent markets and cheap credit.

As a first step, you need to get a clear understanding of all the internal factors that are affecting a situation. This involves talking to internal stakeholders, including senior management, sales, delivery and finance, other market players and even channel partners or alliances in the value chain. This will help in defining and agreeing the goals and measures of success of your marketing activity. After all, to stay on the Fast Track it is important to deliver against the success criteria of your key stakeholders – and that will prove difficult if you don't understand them.

Typical marketing goals can be distilled down to a variant of one of nine options, as defined by the extended Ansoff box derived from the original by Igor Ansoff.[1] This product-market matrix identifies options in terms of selling/marketing existing or new products to existing or new markets and customer segments (see figure).

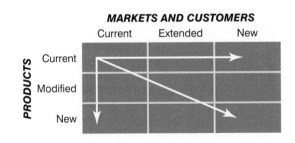

MARKETS AND CUSTOMERS

[1] Ansoff, I. (1957), 'Strategies for diversification', *Harvard Business Review*, 35(5), 113–24.

You will also need to understand the internal constraints that will affect your marketing activity. These might range from strategic issues relating to R&D focus, production capability and financing constraints, to something as simple as stock levels or the sales resources necessary to follow up on leads for a short-term promotion. Of course, time is a constant constraint.

One other constraint is the pool of resources at your disposal. This will certainly affect your choice of activities to develop and implement. But it would also be helpful to understand the criteria that you would need to meet to acquire additional resources. These will probably be financial and will almost certainly be compared against returns that other parts of the business are promising for incremental investment. Only if you can understand and speak finance as the language of business will you be able to compete for such additional resources in order to develop breakthrough marketing returns.

Equally important is an understanding of the external environmental and competitive factors that shape your markets and that you are hoping to influence in turn with your activities. These range from market share and growth rates, probably obtained from industry analysts, to typical market response rates to activities. They will include the expectations and requirements of the target customers, but will also take account of trends, marketing tools and the ways in which your customers access information and make buying decisions. For example, it would be crazy not to understand that customers nowadays don't browse in shops – they browse on the internet, then go into shops and salerooms armed with product, price and competitor information. Who among us would go into a shop to make a major purchase such as a TV or high-end digital camera without first doing research on comparative products and prices through manufacturer websites, review sites and Amazon?

Understanding is not about formal research and analysis, although they certainly contribute, but about having the relevant knowledge on hand to be the basis of decision making and planning. The Fast Track manager will not only always understand the goals and environment of the marketing game in play, but will also have formal and informal systems in place to keep current with any changes to them.

3 PROCESS _Develop_

The development phase is about actionable planning and the strategic or tactical choices and targets that surround that. The Fast Track manager builds that development phase from the understanding phase that goes before it, incorporating basic marketing principles to ensure a solid base for action plans.

At the strategic level choices will depend on factors such as market position and market growth. Many models exist to provide guidance on these options and will be explored when we discuss portfolios (see page 47). At the tactical level choices tend to revolve around which type of programme to implement, which we will look at in more depth in the section on programmes (see page 57).

At both the strategic and individual level there are likely to be several ways of achieving the goals identified, given the constraints, resources and competitive environment. The choices on offer involve different combinations of risk, reward and effectiveness. Sometimes it is blindingly obvious which route to take; on other occasions several viable alternative options will present themselves, so it is important to be able to select the strongest. A simple approach such as the generic V-SAFE screening process can identify the best route forward:

→ **Value.** Does the option deliver tangible benefits, and specifically how likely is it to meet current goals?

→ **Suitable.** Is it consistent with strategy and the status quo?

→ **Acceptable.** Will stakeholders support it and is it an acceptable approach in the external environment?

→ **Feasible.** Are there sufficient resources and time?

→ **Enduring.** Will the idea deliver value in both the long and the short term?

The action plan will flesh out the selected option, incorporating detailed budgets, timelines and task breakdowns. This will form the basis for the project and programme management of the marketing activity.

The key element of the actionable plan is to ensure that you define SMART targets. SMART objectives are:

→ **Specific.** Are the objectives and goals clear, concise and not subject to interpretation?

→ **Measurable.** You need to be able to measure when objectives are being achieved, but beware the two attractive traps that are commonly experienced. Don't pick objectives because they are easily measured – for example, the number of attendees at a promotional event is commonly used but often bears little relation to the overall value of the event. Objectives drive behaviour, so inappropriate objectives can lead to less desirable behaviours. In marketing environments this can mean racking up 'leads' regardless of quality, or a fruitless quest for 'bums on seats'.

→ **Agreed.** A fundamental prerequisite for focusing a team and getting it to pull together is having a common, agreed objective. Therefore, in most variants of the SMART acronym, 'agreed' has a key part to play. This requires the objectives to be understood by all the stakeholders after a degree of discussion and debate. Ultimately all concerned must agree to the objectives in order to get the full commitment of people and resources within the team and other stakeholders.

→ **Realistic.** Are the objectives realistic, given the resource and time constraints?

→ **Time bound.** Are the objectives clearly time bound?

The Fast Track manager will incorporate these elements into strategic and tactical market plans to ensure that all stakeholders can clearly see, communicate and execute marketing activities.

4 PROCESS *Execute*

The execution phase is about delivering, and doing so with a perfect balance of passion, precision and attention to detail. If the development phase is about selecting the most effective approach, then the execution phase is about efficient delivery of the plan. Precision and attention to detail from both leadership and team members are essential to deliver excellent programmes. And while creative excellence is always desirable in this delivery, the most important aspect is delivering the business outcomes, on time and within budget.

That means that project and programme management are critically important skills in delivering excellent marketing programmes. Without these core skills, there is no marketing Fast Track. They bring the rigour to ensure that nothing gets forgotten or falls through the cracks.

QUICK TIP *START EVERY PROJECT WITH CLARITY*
A key to successful project execution and delivery is clarity from the outset. This includes the goals that you aim to achieve and how they align with the big picture and other activities. This not only helps with the project rollout but also is particularly important to provide a steer when the inevitable unforeseen issues arise.

Ideally the marketing team will be using tools to support project and programme delivery. Even a medium-sized marketing team is probably working on several hundred separate marketing activities, which all need to be project managed. The team and management need help to keep track of that amount of work. Even more important, they need early warnings of deviations from the plan, and the ability to replan to accommodate the inevitable changes and issues that arise.

Execution is also the phase where creative skills can get expressed. Obvious areas for creativity include the design and production of communications materials such as adverts, web content and video. But creativity coupled with empowerment also allows team members to manage marketing situations more effectively. Whether dealing with a customer on a telemarketing call or reacting to a difficult and unexpected situation at an event, quick, creative thinking can make the difference between good and great.

Project management skills are needed to meet expectations, but passion and commitment from team members are also required to consistently exceed expectations. So always bear in mind that the Fast Track is dependent on some of the softer management skills as well as on tools and processes.

5 PROCESS Review

The final process phase of review is the area where Fast Track managers can really differentiate themselves. All too often in the rush and pressure of day-to-day marketing activity this final, loop-closing phase gets skipped or short-changed. The temptation to focus on the next upcoming project, with only a cursory assessment of the previous activity, is understandable. Events are a typical example where a quick headcount and review of feedback forms serve to close the project. However, this is a missed opportunity.

A more thorough review and evaluation at the end of the marketing activity brings many benefits. It is an opportunity to assess how the activity delivered against overall goals and activity objectives. Of course, this is so much easier and pertinent if you have already set relevant and SMART objectives during the develop phase.

This assessment of performance against objectives is not a performance management issue but rather an opportunity to learn. How effective was the activity in driving towards our goals? With hindsight, did we pick the right approach or would we do things differently if we had the chance? How efficiently did we deliver the activity? If we were to do it again, would we select a different venue, target different media, alter our messages or aim for a different audience?

The activity might have gone significantly over budget, which on the face of it is bad for the project. But perhaps it was a conscious management decision, taken for very good reasons that we would do again, and therefore needs to be factored into future budgets. Plans, after all, are simply best-guess guides to how to deliver, and anything we can add from experience to improve them should be taken. Best practice only stays relevant if we actively keep it current with latest experience and learning.

The review is about learning from the decisions taken during the three earlier phases of the process so that next time is even more successful. In order for the review to deliver lasting value, the Fast Track manager needs to capture the learning and insights so that they are available for future team activities. Ideally this should be done within the project support environment so that it is readily accessible to all team members.

The Fast Track manager closes each marketing activity with a final review. It doesn't need to be a long formal process, but it does need to evaluate the end results and the key aspects of what went well and what could be improved. These insights can then be fed back into any or all of the earlier phases, to reassess and improve the cycle.

6 PORTFOLIO MANAGEMENT

The Fast Track marketing manager will actively manage a number of portfolios and so an understanding of the basics of portfolio management is useful. You will probably need to direct portfolios of products or brands at different stages of their life cycle and market position. It is likely you will have portfolios of audiences, including customer segments, prospects and influencers, that you will aim to address in turn with a portfolio of complementary propositions and messages.

Rather than jumping into the heavy management theory on portfolios, it's important to take a step back and try 'to see the wood for the trees'. After all, that's really why it is useful to think about portfolios, so that we can see different elements in context. The individual elements need to be managed actively as stand-alone components, but someone such as the Fast Track manager also needs to look at the big picture of how these elements interact and play as a whole.

In fact marketing programme portfolios are not covered extensively in management theory, which is slightly surprising. Programmes tend to develop from goals and objectives in a serial or hierarchical manner. But this development also needs some portfolio thinking, to understand how the programmes support each other to achieve multiple goals or indeed how some might be creating unnecessary duplication. Integrated marketing aligns multiple elements together – such as sponsorship, PR, advertising, web presence, retail competitions and in-store promotions – so that the sum is greater than the parts. But this approach is still linear. Only when you look at the portfolio of goals and programmes, ideally within a support environment that facilitates alignment, can the Fast Track manager fully appreciate the interplay between stand-alone programmes and any duplicates and opportunities for leverage.

Too often, businesses run marketing programmes to customers and targets that at best overlap and at worst conflict. Taking a banking example, you can get a letter from your bank saying that no money has been paid into your account for three months and asking whether you need to discuss this with them, and the following day another mailshot arrives offering to lend you more money. Then you get another one offering life insurance and so on. There is not enough coordination here and the banks are wasting money by bombarding you with direct mail, irrespective of your actual needs and wants.

You will probably have a number of audiences to address with different messages and propositions. These audiences – including target customer segments, channel partners and influencers such as press or industry analysts – can again be managed as a portfolio. Across the portfolio, some messages and propositions will be tailored to specific audiences while others will support a communication with multiple audiences. These variations are usually catered for in a structured message architecture, which can be used as a means to manage the interplay between the two portfolios of audiences and messages.

So a bank might position itself broadly as a listening bank or a local bank, but tailor specific messages to business customers. These business customer messages are then further structured around, for example, larger, multinational businesses requiring international facilities and local SME businesses that need simple and more cost-effective banking.

Finally, consider products and brands, elements that are more commonly viewed as part of portfolios. Well-established tools and approaches such as the Boston Consulting Group (BCG) matrix below can be used to classify products as 'rising stars' or 'cash cows' and such like.

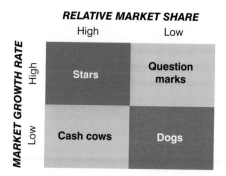

SOURCE: BOSTON CONSULTING GROUP (1970), REPRODUCED WITH PERMISSION.

This four-box matrix defines products or brands by high and low market growth rates and high and low market share. The cut-off between the two can be set arbitrarily, such as 10 per cent growth rate, or more appropriately, it may be set in relation to your market conditions.

→ **Dogs are products or brands in a weak position with low market share and low growth.** They will generate little in terms of margin and presence and will probably even cost money to keep. The theory suggests they should be dropped.

→ **Question marks pose the question of whether or not to invest and develop.** They have low market share, but are in an attractive, growth market that might be worth investing in.

→ **Stars are the headline products that generate a lot of revenue.** However, they also require investment to maintain market share in a competitive growth market.

→ **Cash cows are products in a low growth or even shrinking market that is unlikely to attract new competition, but in which you have a high or even dominant market share.** They generate large positive cash flows since little investment is needed in either product development or marketing to maintain position.

These are useful classifications but don't necessarily provide a complete picture. While they indicate the distribution of products by market share and market growth, that is not enough in today's fast-changing markets. The McKinsey/GE matrix is more thorough in identifying the market and capability characteristics that define the portfolio (see figure). However, both approaches were originally developed to model business units and perhaps lack the more dynamic aspects needed to manage products and brands. Portfolios of products have to address the needs of multiple segments and cater for emerging and existing trends. Products might be needed in embryonic markets that are still ill-defined but nevertheless require a presence. As an innovative business, you might even be creating markets that currently don't exist. These are some of the dynamics that management of the product portfolio should address.

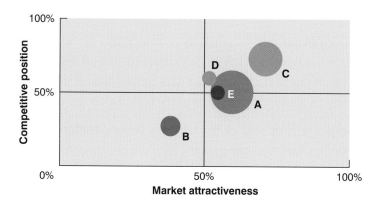

While the BCG matrix is useful to summarise a market position and corresponding marketing emphasis, the McKinsey/GE matrix offers a far more powerful perspective in terms of ability to compete, attractiveness of the market opportunity and its relative size. Always try to make the extra effort to do the fuller analysis required of the McKinsey matrix so that you can benefit from its more dynamic, multi-dimensional outlook. While both these approaches are used as business strategy tools, remember that this is no reason not to use them to benefit marketing thinking. The Director's Toolkit (see pages 183 and 191) offers a more in-depth look at analysing the attractiveness of product and market portfolios.

To summarise, the idea behind viewing groups or clumps as portfolios is simply to get marketing teams to think about managing them in a more active manner. You might have the opportunity to build the portfolio from the ground up or you might inherit a collection, but either way the important thing is to manage them as a whole. A team manager needs each player to perform, but they must also look at the composition of the team as a whole, balancing strengths and weaknesses. Similarly, portfolio management aims to get the best from each element at the same time as assessing its contribution to the overall portfolio. The aim is to make the sum greater than the parts. Sometimes combinations and interactions bring out that extra bit of value or performance, whether it's in marketing programmes or in a sporting context – for example, with a particular Ryder Cup golf pairing.

So the various portfolios should be comprised of elements that are actively balanced by the Fast Track manager. Just as with a financial investment portfolio, marketing portfolios need to be built and then nurtured, pruned, balanced and orchestrated at regular intervals.

QUICK TIP *GET USED TO PORTFOLIOS*

Get into the habit of looking at things as portfolios. We are surrounded by all sorts of portfolios, from iPod playlists to stock market investments, to the composition of teams. The more you view these as portfolios, the easier you will see how to balance the factors involved: risk versus return, or competitive position versus market attractiveness.

---

7 POSITIONING
Inside-out thinking and positioning

Since the early 1960s marketers have been using the four Ps of product, price, promotion and placement as a model for the marketing mix. This is still a valuable thought process but we can now add more to it.

1 **Product**. This defines the specifications, features and benefits of the actual product, as well as the augmented elements surrounding it, such as services, warranties, delivery and financing.

2 **Price**. This defines the market price of the product – the price that the consumer pays and one that defines the margin for the business.

3 **Promotion**. This element is all too often mistaken for the marketing effort itself. It defines the mix of programmes, including advertising, PR, sales promotions, web activity, collaterals, telemarketing and direct marketing that the business uses to promote the product and communicate with audiences.

4 **Placement**. This defines the sales channels that the business decides upon to deliver the offering to the market. Recently, of course, this has moved on from direct sales or one and two-tier channel models to include online sales. This in turn opens a world of geographic markets. Amazon, for example, only actually operates in five countries, but it markets and ships globally.

Positioning is the result of these marketing mix decisions. But the model does have limitations, despite its universal understanding and use. Many people believe that the model is best suited to simpler marketing environments, such as low-value or fast-moving consumer goods (FMCG), rather than, for example, the more complex, multi-dimensional interactions of industrial markets. It has been suggested that you actually need seven Ps to describe a full marketing mix, although there isn't always unanimous agreement as to precisely what those extra three Ps are. Whether these are people, process, provision of service or physical attributes (such as design), together they more fully capture the essence of the offering and how it is packaged and delivered to the market. Services marketing is certainly more easily described by a seven Ps model.

Each of the four elements outlined above is itself the subject of whole books, describing the detailed interactions, theories and best practice. Each of the elements has its own collection of tools, techniques and approaches to get to the answers. But essentially it is another perspective on how to break down the strategic thinking behind the marketing plan. So any marketing plan should incorporate some four Ps thinking in just the same way as you would include some level of SWOT analysis.

These frameworks have proved very useful to marketers over the years. But they all suffer from the same inherent fault, which was less of an issue when operating in the simpler markets of the past. Whether the model has four or seven Ps, the fact is that they are all approaching tasks from the inside out. They have an internal perspective, about what capabilities are being configured in products and margins and promotional marketing activities. None of the thinking is from the customer or market perspective, i.e. from the outside in. This has become more of an issue in the intensely competitive markets of today, when buyers have the ability to meet their wants and needs through a number of different sources.

So marketing needs a mix model that asks the questions from the other way round. One example is the SIVA model. This takes a customer perspective and instead of product, promotion, price and place, it asks about solutions, information, value and access. However, this can become an exercise in semantics, since although it frames it more from the customer angle it is still basically the same model:

→ solution replaces product

→ information replaces promotion

→ value replaces price

→ access replaces place.

But there's much more. You really have to put yourself into the moccasins of the customer, think about the problem from a different angle and move on to step 8.

8 POSITIONING
Outside-in thinking and positioning

I'm not suggesting that we dispense with the four or seven Ps, but simply that we add another dimension to our thinking as marketers so that we can engage much more effectively with our audiences. It's not just about tinkering with words, but also about taking another, more encompassing view. The four Rs add to the previous models by bringing concepts of relevance, receptivity, responsiveness and relationship to our thinking. These ideas cut through the inside-out thinking and supplement it with more interactive approaches.

Relevance is fairly self-explanatory. It's about communicating with customers through content and media that are meaningful for them and that resonate with them. At the simplest level relevance is addressing customer issues with solutions and benefits as opposed to features and specifications. This is outside-in thinking, taking the customer viewpoint rather than your own. One of the key relevance tools is value. In B2B and B2C (business-to-consumer) markets customers are receptive to the concept of value as long as it's their value. Every marketing activity or communication you undertake needs to pass the relevance test. In these days of message bombardment and attention deficits, only relevant messages have any chance of getting through. The more relevant the communication, the more **receptive** the audience is likely to be and the greater the chances that you will get the response that you are seeking.

Timing is the other key to receptivity. Even the most relevant message or positioning statement needs to arrive at the right time if it is to be acted upon. Inputs may be rejected, embraced or very often noted as interesting for some other time. So it's important to recognise that you will probably need to deliver many relevant messages in order to engage with a target audience and develop a relationship. If you can keep all communication relevant and of value, then audiences will still be receptive – whether or not the time is right for action.

QUICK TIP *KEEP ASKING 'SO WHAT?'*
Outside-in thinking is helped by a regular test of 'So what?' in marketing thinking. Take the time to stop and put yourself in the customer's position and ask 'So what?' so that the team doesn't get caught up in an internal perspective. Gillette provides a great example: so what if the Fusion razor has got 16 patents and five blades, does it actually make a tangible difference to the user?

Responsiveness is a two-way street. The business needs to be responsive to the needs and trends within the market and to specific customer feedback. This works on several levels, from responding to wider market trends, such as pricing or sustainability, to being seen to be responsive to a distressed customer contacting a call centre. But as marketers you are also aiming to develop responsiveness from your markets and customers. Marketing teams need to be thinking about the response they are trying to engender from customers and markets with every interaction. This might range from triggering emotions, such as 'I want one' or 'I feel comfortable that I bought that model because it's the best value on the market' or 'That's interesting', through to targeted action responses, including 'Call now to secure your pre-release order'.

References and referrals are the next step towards establishing lasting **relationships** with customers and markets. Referrals also come into effect at different levels. Referees don't even need to be actual customers; they just need to have engaged with your brand. Whether that engagement is a childhood poster of a dream car, a chance product sampling or an integrated sponsorship of your favourite sport, it is the start of an emotional link. Experiential marketing aims to bring some flavour of the proposition experience to customers, prospects and other influencers, including press or channels. Tools in the experiential arsenal include events and hospitality, product sampling, 'stunts' or any of a broad range of activities with an entertaining or educational content. Of course, referrals also come from satisfied customers, either consciously or unconsciously. A friend might introduce you to their favourite brand of coffee or beer, not necessarily with a buy recommendation but just to be hospitable. Getting to the point where customers will endorse or advocate your offering is the start of a valuable relationship.

Relationships are one of the main objectives of marketing. Relationship marketing has been viewed for a while as a sub-category that applies more to high-value goods and services. But that's rubbish. For a start, it's not a sub-category, it is the essence of marketing. Even commodity products aim to develop relationships between the brand and the consumer. Nescafé and Kenco aim to develop relationships with coffee drinkers, while Shell and BP want drivers to routinely select their pumps. Whether they are trying to differentiate the brand in a commodity market or simply establish a level of comfort or trust, they are aiming to forge an enduring relationship. Obviously, as the value of the purchase increases, this relationship can become more important, even if purchases are less frequent. Rolex seeks to establish long-term relationships with customers by associating itself with their actual or inspirational lifestyles through the sponsorship of sailing, motor racing, tennis, golf and culture. BMW takes a multi-level approach to developing relationships through marketing with a combination of sponsorship, events, communications and advertising over and above its product and service proposition. We are talking about more than the buzzword of relationship marketing and the concepts of customer relationship marketing (CRM), which again are inside-out concepts. What we are talking about here is the situation where customers truly feel that they have and want a relationship with your business.

For example, Volvo sponsors sailing races (rather than, say, Formula One) because it believes values associated with that sport are closer to the ideals of the company than the more obvious alternative of motor racing. According to Volvo's website: 'Harnessing the natural elements of wind and wave power, sailing and Volvo make the ideal match; the brand's three core values of quality, environmental care and safety enshrined in a world-class sailing portfolio.'

In the end, relationships endure while transactions don't, so everything that marketing does should ultimately be focused on delivering 'sticky' relationships with customers in target markets.

Although there is an argument that the four Rs and experiential marketing focus too much on the emotional responses and feelings of customers, when these are combined with rational drivers such as value or the output of the four Ps then they become highly compelling.

9 PROGRAMME CHOICES

Marketing plans come to life through programmes that implement a range of activities to bring the four Ps and the four Rs of your offering to the market. Your choice of programme activities can very well make the difference between successfully achieving your objectives and using up valuable time and resources on a learning exercise.

A marketing programme should really pull together a number of elements in an integrated approach, where the sum is greater than the parts. A one-dimensional advertising series, even with multiple ads, is a far less powerful approach than an integrated programme that approaches the market from several angles. This section introduces some successful, growth programme types that are proving popular with small and large organisations alike and which you should always consider within your programme mix.

When speaking to business audiences, the UK managing director of Amazon offers some simple advice. Embrace the **internet** or prepare to get fit for a career as an item picker in an Amazon dispatch warehouse. The world first glimpsed the internet revolution with the dotcom boom at the turn of the century, but only with the advent of Web 2.0 concepts has the true impact really started to become apparent. And many will say that this is still just the start. But already it has got to the point where no marketing programme should get past the first planning stage without an online element. This may not be the only element, nor even necessarily the main element, but it will certainly be an integrated part of the picture.

Whether advertising with carefully chosen keywords on Google or Facebook, creating tailored landing pages, engaging with communities using blogs, harnessing the power of social networks or using online viral marketing, the internet provides access to vast audiences. The numbers are not only large but also highly segmented. The web encompasses every segment of human behaviour you could think of, but each of those segments is a vibrant, active and potentially large niche. You have no choice but to embrace the internet and the cost-effective access it provides to audiences and communities.

The explosive fragmentation of this online world makes the job of the marketer even more critical, because targeting your audience and your message becomes increasingly important. Traditional segmentation models and approaches are ever more strained, putting more emphasis on getting the basics right.

While not able to match the stellar growth of the online world, **sponsorship** is another high-growth marketing platform that offers lots of advantages over more traditional approaches such as above-the-line advertising. Sponsorships tend to be multi-dimensional from the outset, offering many ways and levels to work with and access audiences. Typically, the rights negotiated as part of a deal will allow sponsors to develop awareness, drive preference and build relationships with customers, prospects, channels and influencers, all at the same time. The power of the sponsorship platform is such that it will deliver against several goals and imperatives – as long as you activate and exploit the opportunity appropriately.

Notable and highly successful sponsorships include Kingfisher's support for yachtswoman Ellen MacArthur via their B&Q and Castorama brands, and the extensive portfolio of Red Bull sponsorships that target a wide section of the youth audience. Both these examples were and are used to build brand presence and awareness and to develop a large range of relationships. Such relationships might be with employees, channels, suppliers, influencers, existing customers and prospect targets. These are just two examples of how sponsorship, when done properly, is a very powerful marketing tool that delivers in multiple dimensions against a wide range of objectives and audiences.

One of the key aspects of a sponsorship is that it starts to engage with audiences at an emotional level much earlier than traditional approaches. It gives back to the audience in a way that advertising can never hope to achieve. (This is not to say that you wouldn't also then integrate advertising into the sponsorship activation plan.) However, just because there is this emotional engagement, you shouldn't assume that sponsorship only works for consumer audiences: far from it. There are many examples of successful sponsorships in B2B and industrial markets. Whether you are a technology company demonstrating how your solution can make a Formula One team more agile and responsive, or a services business sponsoring golf or tennis or sailing, you can craft a sponsorship to deliver against the four Rs, so that target audiences can start to experience your proposition. Again, because of the explosion of media channels, including the web, sponsorship can be accurately targeted to specific groups, although media exposure, of course, is only one of the many elements that a sponsorship delivers.

Sponsorship continues to be dominated by sport. However, there is significant growth in entertainment and music, and to a lesser extent broadcast sponsorship (which is still a minor player, despite the apparent popularity of certain TV properties). Many of these are large, multimillion pound deals, but equally sponsorship applies to smaller budgets with more modest goals in terms of market impact and relationship development. So don't be put off: explore how sponsorship could be used to achieve your marketing aims.

Experiential and guerrilla marketing are two popular concepts that use the web and sponsorship to a greater or lesser extent. They provide fresh and interactive ways to communicate with audiences and offer marketers effective programmes to achieve a variety of objectives.

With escalating fragmentation and shortening attention spans, **experiential marketing** offers an increasingly important way for marketing and the business to engage with target audiences. The thinking is to provide relevant and memorable ways to make a connection, with examples ranging from product sampling, through PR stunts to sponsorship activation and even custom, company-owned events such as the Red Bull Flug-Tag. Here audiences get to experience the personality of the brand and hence have the chance to develop a much closer connection than would be the case after seeing an advert or receiving a piece of mail, whether through the post or on email. By triggering an emotional link, backed up by more traditional, rational features and benefits attributes, businesses can use experiential approaches to get a sustainable advantage in attracting prospective customers and enhancing the loyalty of existing customers.

Guerrilla marketing, as the name suggests, uses a selection of tactical, cost-effective marketing weapons to create high returns and impact through sustained 'attacks'. Perhaps frowned upon by high-brow marketers, guerrilla marketing nevertheless has many appealing attributes.

While planned, ongoing marketing programmes are obviously the pre-ferred course, guerrilla marketing activity can be quickly activated or scrapped, depending on budgets and programme results. Well suited to smaller businesses and their budgets, activities will use a series of cre-ative ideas that take time, energy and imagination rather than money, which punch above their weight to create those important relationships and connections.

Whichever way you prefer to look at them, these four programme types deliver strong platforms for integrated marketing programmes, which you should investigate and incorporate into your plans.

10 PERFORMANCE MANAGEMENT

Managing marketing performance has become a critical element of the discipline in recent years and is set to stay that way. Both management and measurement take place at several levels: from the strategic and financial impact on the business to the key performance indicators (KPIs) for any particular activity.

Earlier, the review phase of the marketing process established the learning and measurement practices that take place as the conclusion to all marketing activities. These will include KPIs and the SMART objectives identified in the planning phase of the activity. These measurements establish the effectiveness and efficiency of the tactical execution, which is an important element of marketing performance management. The measurements might include attendees at events, leads, click-throughs or advertising value equivalents (AVE). But it's important to measure the things that matter and drive the business rather than just those that are easy to measure. AVE is a commonly used PR metric that is actually a very poor measurement of the success of a PR programme, because all it does is compare coverage to the amount of advertising spend to get the same exposure. So it is a measure, but it is not really very meaningful in terms of how to improve the performance of PR, marketing or the busi-ness. Even when you are measuring the correct tactical outputs, you still have to coordinate them to ensure that performance management is driv-ing the business in the right direction.

These tactical effectiveness measures should help marketing teams when deciding the allocation of resources for future programmes. Which type of activity in the given circumstance is most effective at delivering against the marketing objectives? Obviously this can be a simple choice between a live, face-to-face sales seminar or a web-based event that can address a much larger audience at less cost. Alternatively, it might involve complex considerations around a multifaceted and multilayered sponsorship programme and associate activation and exploitation.

Marketing leaders now also need to be literate in the language of finance in order to express marketing returns in terms that the purse-holders and senior management understand. As we move away from the tactical execution of programmes to the overall impact of marketing on the business, we need a different set of metrics and measurement to support high-level decision making. It might be possible to articulate success in terms of a return on marketing investment (ROMI), or perhaps at a lower-level return on sponsorship investment, but to a large extent these are measures of efficiency. Perhaps a better approach is to express results as returns against objectives, but this will require an understanding not only of financial terminology but also of how the hard, bottom-line figures of the business relate to those marketing objectives. There is an argument that the finance team should develop and own the marketing metrics with support from marketing. Either way, marketers need to be fluent in the language of business finance to be taken seriously by the business.

When the marketing team at BA developed a dashboard to manage marketing performance, they worked on four key principles: tie measures to strategy; distil measures down to a small set of metrics; ensure stakeholder buy-in; and tie metrics to the decision-making process. From hundreds of initial measures the dashboard was eventually reduced to nine metrics that truly reflected the business at that time. These nine metrics covered the four categories of financial performance, customer relationships, brand health and internal efficiency, which were supplemented by premium market share, channel mix, uptake of e-services, customer satisfaction marketing spend versus budget, and key revenue figures. All these directly relate to BA business objectives and strategies.

The trick is to identify and get stakeholder buy-in for a set of metrics that bridges the gap between the marketers implementing the activities and the senior, board-level management decision makers. In order to be effective at managing marketing performance, the metrics need to be relevant and meaningful at both levels of the business.

Once metrics are agreed, if the right tools and systems are in place, performance management should become a matter of standard practice. Given that the review phase should be an integral part of the marketing process, the metrics can then be monitored, using Red-Amber-Green flags, throughout the programme development and implementation. It sounds too simple to be true, but if you get the basics right, it can be!

A number of good books tackle this critical subject – for example, *Marketing and the Bottom Line* by Tim Ambler and *Marketing Metrics* by Farris, Bendle, Pfeifer and Reibstein.[2] Take time to get familiar with the basics: it has only been by talking this language of business that marketing leaders have become more widely accepted on management boards around the world. Make sure you are fluent in this language to support your claim to the Fast Track.

STOP – THINK – ACT

After reading this chapter you will have learned about a variety of best practice tools and techniques used by some of the world's most successful companies to optimise their marketing performance. Some will be more relevant to you than others, and some may need to be adapted to suit your specific situation. Take time now to reflect on the top ten marketing tools and techniques, and identify the elements that you will include in your marketing framework.

What should we do?	What tools and techniques are appropriate?
Who do we need to involve?	Who needs to be involved and why?
What resources will we require?	What information, facilities, materials, equipment or budget will be required?
What is the timing?	How long will each activity typically take?

Visit **www.Fast-Track-Me.com** to use the Fast Track online planning tool.

---

[2] Ambler, Tim (2003), *Marketing and the Bottom Line*, Harlow: Pearson Education; Farris, Paul W., Bendle, Neil T., Pfeifer, Phillip E. and Reibstein, David J. (2007), *Marketing Metrics*, Philadelphia: Wharton School Publishing.

Successful brand building means evoking history – the case of the Olympic Games

Practice Associate Professor John A. Davis

Imagine legions of loyal customers telling succeeding generations stories of the greatness of your brand, magnifying its accomplishments, with the resulting halo casting an angelic glow over all that your company touches, rendering problems, scandals and crises to footnote status. Sounds implausible in this age of painful scrutiny over every mistake companies make? Perhaps not, when one views the brand through the lens of history and, in particular, the Olympic Games, as I discuss in depth in my book *The Olympic Games Effect: How Sports Marketing Builds Strong Brands*.[3]

Marketing, if nothing else, is about developing, building and sustaining a positive reputation for the entity being marketed in the hopes that others will find the entity compelling enough to support it. In the modern era, this support is in the form of profitable, loyal customers. The Olympic Games of the Ancient Greek world built a remarkable legacy of reputable success that lasted for 1,200 years, yet they were not marketed, at least not in the modern sense of marketing. The Games were an integral part of Greek life, known for attracting the best athletes, competing and representing their home city-state for the honour and glory of being an Olympic champion. Victors received rewards, including free food for life, new homes and tax-free status. Victory and the ensuing fame, therefore, were certainly sought. Olympic success and the subsequent notoriety undoubtedly helped foster positive reputations for those involved, spreading the Olympic message through an ancient form of viral marketing – word of mouth. The stories of Olympic competition provided instructive lessons on the virtues of dedication to cause, translated through the tradition of storytelling in which tales of Olympic athletic achievement were spread from one generation to the next, inspiring images of victory and dreams of eternal glory.

'Holding an Olympic Games means evoking history,' said Baron Pierre de Coubertin, the founder of the modern Olympics.[4] This is a grand, perhaps even daunting sentiment. Evoking history implies a significant responsibility,

[3] Davis, J.A. (2008), *The Olympic Games Effect: How Sports Marketing Builds Strong Brands*, Chichester: John Wiley & Sons.
[4] Blais, Eric (2007), 'Quebec and 2010', *Marketing Magazine*, 112 (21).

and less majestically, a great burden is placed on those that attempt to carry out such lofty ambitions. Failure by any city and its Olympic planners to recognise the importance of the Olympic Games and then organise resources to ensure success risks eternal historical infamy. Given this risk, why do so many companies and cities today vie for a chance to be involved with the Olympic Games? The answer lies partly in understanding the origins of the Games, since even a rudimentary review will provide a better sense of the traditions and historical context that have helped shape the Olympic reputation as it exists today. Additionally, there is the magnetic attraction of the Olympic Dream – a concept loaded with imagery and associations like 'authenticity', 'mythology', 'mystique' and 'the pinnacle of sport' that are simultaneously positive, motivating and virtuous.

For host cities and corporate sponsors, the premier status of the Olympics offers a unique and highly credible event that captures the imagination of the world and casts a remarkable halo effect over the stakeholders involved. This is not to suggest that the Olympics are without fault, because there are well-documented examples of scandals and improprieties that violate the Olympic spirit and rules of conduct that, as a consequence, risk tarnishing the event's reputation and harm the commercial interests of the IOC's (International Olympic Committee) key corporate sponsors. But interestingly, the scandals have not caused irreparable harm (yet), which suggests that the Olympics enjoy such an exalted status in the eyes of the public that they are willing to forgive short-term transgressions if the integrity of the actual athletic competitions themselves remains intact. Imagine your company enjoying a similar Teflon reputation (of course, ongoing scandals would be increasingly hard to overcome, so the onus is on the IOC to ensure the highest possible integrity and rules of conduct for all involved, just as the pressure is on senior management to ensure transparent, ethical business practices for their company).

Companies keen on building and reinforcing an image of trust and integrity invest in sponsoring the Olympics because the event's very authenticity can confer similar credibility on the sponsoring company. This is due to the visibility resulting from the association, not unlike when a person has their photograph taken with a famous person – suddenly, that 'average Joe' gets the notoriety. The sheer novelty of the occasion elevates the unknown temporarily. The challenge is translating this one-time event into longer-term success and benefits. For smart companies, the real advantage of Olympic sponsorship lies in the long-term commitment and associated activities, not the temporary excitement of two weeks of Olympic events. This rationale of supporting a long-term marketing investment is vital to effective and successful marketing efforts. Stopping sponsorship after one Olympics does not enable a company to leverage its investment and/or contribute to a longer-term growth plan. Senior management will always be tempted to cancel any programme that does not demonstrate direct contribution to company performance. Yet, as successful marketers know, one run of an ad campaign, or any other communication, is too limited to gain a complete understanding of the long-term impact. Conversely, switching marketing tactics frequently can confuse the market, undermine company positioning and reputation, and embolden competitors to take advantage of weakness. Think of it from an athlete's point of view: if a top athlete trains for months, or years, and then races once to see whether the training paid off, but retires if he or she loses, then there is little learned. The real benefit comes from altering race techniques and competing repeatedly to see what nuances are required to achieve consistent success.

The key lesson? Examined through the lens of an iconic sports event, we are reminded that dedication to cause, coupled with thoughtful adaptation, is the best approach to successful brand building.

TECHNOLOGIES

To remain as effective and efficient as possible, Fast Track managers differentiate themselves by the support mechanisms they put in place for themselves, their team and their businesses. These include the intelligent use of appropriate technologies – enabling, for example, the automation of non-core activities, thereby freeing up time to focus on managing, motivating and leading people. They may also include the use of coaches and peer-to-peer networks, and gaining access to the latest thinking in their field. Marketing is an area that has especially benefited from developments in information and communication technology in recent years and it would be foolish not to explore the possibilities these offer in terms of cost savings, time to market and other efficiencies.

Getting started

Why consider technology?

Technology is not without its issues, so teams need to make sure the focus is on how technology can improve the delivery of the end result rather than act as an end in its own right. Despite potential detractors and distractions, however, technology offers huge benefits in terms of agility, speed to market and cost efficiency.

Markets are changing dramatically. All industries are seeing consolidation, global competition, dynamic financial and market conditions, and relentless rewriting of legislation. The question is whether technology can help us to keep up or even ahead of this pace of change.

> **QUICK TIP** *BE REALISTIC*
> Use technology where appropriate but don't let it stop you
> from delivering the results you need today. Expect
> implementation times to be longer than promised, so plan for
> getting on with the job at hand. This was an issue with early
> major CRM implementations, where too many programmes
> were put on hold while waiting for the system to deliver.

There is certainly no shortage of information. The problem is how to make sense of the myriad of junk emails, websites, free journals and mobile texts that arrive uninvited at all times of the day and night. While information overload is a critical issue, it's also true that we have never before had such timely access to so much relevant information with which to take on the competition.

So, while technology is not the answer to all our problems, it is a very important enabler to help us remain effective and efficient. When used and applied appropriately, technology can save us time and money, help us communicate easily with widely dispersed audiences and provide easy access to important information both internally and externally.

How do I free up time?

Technology should offer two things to the marketing team. It helps you to save time by automating low-value processes and activity; and it enables you to do things that you previously wouldn't have attempted, generally because of the scale of the task. The simplest example of this is email marketing, whereby you can now quickly and cheaply communicate with tens or even hundreds of thousands of customers or prospects at the touch of a button, as opposed to printing and posting the same number of letters. Ignoring for a moment the issues around data protection and spam email, this is technology enabling a new way of working, with a number of positive and negative consequences.

One of the cornerstones of success in any discipline is an ability to focus on the 'juice', the high-value-added elements that really make the difference. Many people subscribe to the application of the Pareto principle: that 80 per cent of the results come from 20 per cent of your time or effort. The other way of looking at this is that 80 per cent of your efforts only produce 20 per cent of the results, meaning that everyone is actually wasting a lot of time.

One of the key tenets of technology is garbage-in, garbage-out. This applies not only to data input but also to processes. There is no point in automating poor or unnecessary processes and activity. Eliminate or improve them before you try to automate them.

So start by assessing the various activities that you and/or your team are involved in on a regular, week-by-week basis. Make a list (probably quite a long one) of all the tasks, then roughly map them on to this simple two-by-two matrix:

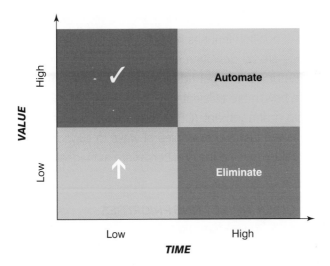

→ Those falling in the bottom right-hand corner are the critical ones to address – they take a lot of time but are adding little **value**. Eliminate these. The drudgery of monthly reporting could be an example here. In theory it is an important management tool, but in practice it wastes a lot of time and creates minimal value. Support systems that utilise project management tools can help to remove the need for teams to construct monthly reports simply by automatic reporting of actual activities, status and outstanding issues.

→ Those in the bottom left-hand corner pose a problem. They are not consuming much time, so are reasonably efficient, but they are not delivering a lot of value. Perhaps there is a way of improving the value of each activity. You might, for example, change the agenda on a weekly operational update meeting to include asking the team to come up with at least one new idea for improvement.

→ **Activities in the top left box are of high value and are not too time consuming.** They would seem to be efficient already, but it's still worth checking whether there is room for improvement. They might already be automated, or be candidates for automation when the right technology solution becomes available at the right price.

→ **The core of the marketing process sits in the top right-hand box.** It can take a lot of thinking and creative iteration to deliver a market position that has huge value to the company, so these activities are by definition important and high value. Although you do not want to get rid of these activities, you do need to explore new, more efficient ways of doing them. Customer relationship management (CRM) and business intelligence (BI) systems are just two examples of ways to support these types of activity by making the numbers more manageable.

QUICK TIP SETTING PRIORITIES
While you are learning to focus on the 'juice', practise some simple approaches to prioritisation. With axes labelled 'important' and 'urgent', create another four-box matrix to help you identify the highly important and urgent items. This will also remind you that important but non-urgent activities should not be put at the bottom of the pile.

Think carefully about your overall time management: be aware of how you use your time and constantly look for ways of improving this. Don't forget that we tend to do those things that we enjoy and put off what is less fun. If you're serious about putting technology to the best possible use, then try to overcome this psychological bias and look at the use of your time as objectively as you can. If you do not manage your time well, you will always be working on the urgent, short-term, visible activities rather than on the overall cycle. It boils down to the old time management test of urgent versus important and the four options this creates (urgent and important, urgent and not important, not urgent and important, not urgent and not important). Don't get stuck in constant cycles of delivering important/urgent activity. Delegate or eliminate the unimportant/ non-urgent activity. Try to focus on the important and manage your time to ensure that these things are done before they become urgent. Trust the voice of experience on this one!

When invited to meetings, constantly ask the question 'Why?' What value will the meeting give you, or what value will you give to it? If there is no obvious answer, then decline the invitation or delegate. The key is to remove unnecessary tasks and activities before looking for opportunities to automate: that way you avoid putting IT and other resources into something that has little or no value.

Finally, encourage your team to carry out the same exercise so that when you are deciding on various options for automation you are aiming to increase the overall effectiveness of the team, not just yourself.

The process-system link

How should we use technology?

Think carefully about how you will use technology and ensure it links back to what you are seeking to achieve. Perhaps the starting point is your overall marketing framework, where you can look for opportunities to make each element quicker, simpler – and possibly more fun!

Some aspects of the framework will lend themselves to the use of technology, whereas some of the softer areas, such as basic principles and positioning, will offer fewer opportunities.

 CASE STORY DELL, STEVE'S STORY

Narrator Steve is a member of the marketing team for Europe, the Middle East and Africa, and is responsible for a wide range of marketing activities and promotions.

Context Dell was founded in 1984 on an idea to sell computer systems directly to customers, cutting out the middle men and offering competitive pricing by passing savings on to customers. One of the earliest businesses to harness the power of the internet to help in connecting to customers, by 2000 Dell had reached online sales of $50 million per day.

Issue Dell has always explored new ways to engage with customers and has now started to work with other distribution channels to address commercial and consumer markets. A number of systems have been put in place to support direct communication with customers via direct mail, email and telephone. However, CRM systems have been implemented primarily from a sales perspective and are not well suited for the needs of marketing.

Solution While it is important to keep a consistent source of customer and prospect data in order to coordinate communications and promotions, Steve and his team decided to develop a single marketing database. This is a sophisticated database with a number of event triggers that initiate communication on customer actions as well as internally driven promotions programmes. However, the database is kept separate from the sales-driven CRM system.

Learning Although the theory states that businesses should have a single view of the customer, the reality is that different parts of the business take a different perspective and need data for their own slightly differing purposes. For Dell, it works to run from different systems, and for Steve and the team to coordinate the sales and marketing activities in other ways.

Top technologies

How do I know what technology exists?

So we now understand the need for technology, systems and automation and where we are going to deploy it for best effect, but how do we find out what is available?

Scan the web for trends in both technology and marketing. You can find plenty of marketing material from vendors offering every imaginable solution, but you will also find many case studies of businesses that have adopted technologies to improve the way they operate. Also look in the marketing press. Again, you will find case examples and technology reviews of what is available. You could also try attending some of the huge number of exhibitions, conferences or seminars available. There are even events specifically on technology in marketing, but make sure that the content is relevant to your type of business, perhaps in terms of size or industry structure.

> QUICK TIP *CHECK OUT MARKETING TECHNOLOGY IN YOUR INDUSTRY*
>
> Try to understand how your competitors and other players in your industry use technology to improve their marketing. You might either spot an opportunity to take a lead or see the chance to stand back and evaluate the impact on their market presence.

Be careful not to get swamped by the volume of information available, and remember that there are new technologies coming along all the time. Start with a healthy scepticism. Investigate the technology, but ask the 'So what?' question – is this relevant to my team and to me, and how will it impact performance? Decide also whether you want to be an early adopter, at the leading edge of marketing technology, or perhaps in the early or late majority, when you can see how the benefits are delivered in other businesses.

What tools will support an efficient and effective marketing function?

There are a few key areas where technology can help marketing teams stay ahead of the game. They either tend to assist communication with audiences – making it cheaper or more efficient to stay in contact – or provide greater understanding of the environment or behaviours. Of course implementing these two drivers together will result in the biggest payback.

By their nature, technologies are changing fast, so it's a good idea to keep up to date with the latest developments that might help with improving the effectiveness and efficiency of your marketing. The following list explores some areas that you should be considering as a start.

1 Customer relationship management (CRM)

What is it?

The Chartered Institute of Marketing defines CRM as 'the coherent management of contacts and interactions with customers'. However, the term is often used to describe the software systems and IT that enable this process. These are a set of applications, built on a database of customer details, that facilitate all types of interaction with customers. The applications include tools to assist sales, marketing, contact centres, web interactions, customer support and service. The CRM system should also interface directly with many of the other technologies in this top ten list.

So whether we are talking about the management process or the systems to support it, the key point is that CRM provides a single, unified view of the customer. This actually means managing the business's interactions with the customer in a coherent and joined-up manner, rather than managing the relationship. We might try to guide the relationship, but let's not fool ourselves that we actually control it. So managing all the interactions with and knowledge of the customer through one system is a huge step forward.

Pros

CRM allows us to accurately and consistently nurture relationships, up-selling and cross-selling in a controlled way, gradually developing a more detailed picture of the customer and their behaviour while attempting to build customer loyalty and value. It offers a powerful insight into the customer and what they get from us, as well as a tool to capture and possibly control our interactions with them. It also acts as a foundation for many other technologies and tools that either provide us with information or help us to enhance or streamline our communications with customers.

Cons

While CRM offers many benefits, some implementations have fallen foul of over-promising and under-delivering. It is easy to expect and demand too much of the systems, letting the scope of initial implementation grow too large. Many early implementations took years and millions of pounds before going live, late and over budget, to a sceptical internal audience. The trick is probably to start small and plan to grow both data volumes and scope later.

Success factors

The key is to try to keep the CRM systems as compact and unobtrusive as possible, while delivering all the benefits of coordination described above. CRM technology is a means to an end, not an end in its own right, so it should support rather than get in the way of internal sales and marketing teams as well as the actual interactions with customers. Again, the most successful approach is to carefully limit the initial system rather than reaching for the sky, and then grow that system as the benefits and opportunities are established. Success will also depend on the accuracy with which information is captured. Technology can't work miracles: if you put rubbish into the system, that's probably what you should expect to get out.

2 The web

What is it?

The internet is simply a huge interconnected network of computers based on a common set of technical standards that lets them communicate easily with each other. On top of this raw network of computing power is the World Wide Web, again based on a set of interoperability standards, which offers billions of linked web pages representing vast amounts of knowledge and material. This network is the technology foundation on which many of the other top ten technologies listed here are based.

It almost needs a whole chapter to explain the role of the web and the internet, so great are their impact. The web has become a shop window for you to display or even sell your offerings to customers. At the same time you can use it as a research tool to investigate competitive offerings either directly on their websites (just as they can with your site) or through third parties. E-commerce systems that can interface with your CRM system are used to buy, sell and transact with customers, suppliers or partners, making the web more dynamic. Web users can opt to 'pull' information by browsing or have information 'pushed' to them through newsfeeds, RSS feeds and podcasts that provide updates on the latest developments and news for every imaginable topic. These range from weather and surf reports to stock prices and industry news. This same internet/web technology can also be used within the business through an intranet.

Pros

The web provides a rich source of information on an infinite variety of topics. The information is often free and you can get hold of it very fast, providing a wealth of detail about customers and competitors in a matter of minutes where previously it would have taken weeks. As well as information provision, the web also facilitates a wide range of communications and a new revenue stream in the form of electronic commerce.

You can also use the web to publish your own information and messages to the world. For this, you need to be familiar with search engine optimisation (SEO) and Google ads and the like, as well as techniques for attracting people to your site to hear your messages.

Cons

The scale and richness of the web brings some potential downsides. While stimulating creativity and exploration, it can lead to a lack of focus and difficulty in finding the definitive answer. The US journalist Franklin P. Adams said, 'I find that a great part of the information I have was acquired by looking up something and finding something else on the way.' So it is a very powerful tool but one that needs to be used with some direction and an enquiring mind. It also needs to be remembered that much of the information contains a degree of bias – after all, someone has produced it for their own purposes. The information might be marketing material, individual opinions or simply innocent but inaccurate data.

Success factors

The web can be used as a rich source of knowledge, and so mechanisms should be set up to review competitor and customer information regularly. Processes and systems should also be developed to maximise the communications and commerce opportunities offered by this technology. But beware of information overload. And if you are using information for making critical decisions, then validate your conclusions using other sources. A neat rule of thumb is the one that journalists use – only publish a 'fact' if you have got at least two reliable sources.

Take time to understand how your target audiences use the web to find information, for entertainment and to make purchase decisions. Harness that knowledge to make sure not only that they can find you among the billions of sites out there, but also that they stay for a while because of the value and interest you offer.

3 Telephony solutions

What are they?

Despite developments in IT such as the internet, many customers still want to talk to somebody, just as they actually want to shop face to face. Telephony technologies and solutions address a wide range of areas, including contact and call centres where customer calls are handled in a mass-production process. Other applications are customer self-service solutions such as interactive voice response (IVR) and automated enquiry systems, which remove the need to staff the other end of the phone. When linked with CRM solutions, such telephony applications enable effective mass-market telemarketing, both inbound and outbound.

Pros

When used properly, telephony technologies can transform the customer experience and even the company proposition. Just consider the success and customer satisfaction demonstrated by First Direct. Telephony technologies enable the business to deal efficiently with customer sales and service calls, support outbound customer contact and allow a consistently high level of service, which translates to very high loyalty, retention and recommendation rates.

Cons	The potential pitfalls are all too familiar. When the emphasis is biased towards cost savings rather than experience, customers can be subjected to frustrating delays, menu options and queues, rigid scripts and poorly trained customer service staff. And that is before we consider the typical customer reaction to off-shore contact centres.
Success factors	As with many technologies, the difference between getting telephony right and wrong can be huge. The trick is to accept that technologies enable new ways of working but they are not a panacea. You have to use them to improve the business: it's no good saving money through a contact centre if by doing so you drive away profitable customers. Telephony technology is one of the areas where it is easy to understand this, since we have all probably experienced the best and worst that it offers.

4 Email marketing

What is it?	Email marketing, when done properly and linked to systems such as CRM, automates mass communication with customers but with a personal touch. Email marketing can be a cost-effective way for the business to stay in the forefront of a customer's mind. The emails can take an informative or sales-oriented tone, since customers accept information in this form as adding value to their businesses or lifestyles.
Pros	It is a cheap and effective way to engage with customers on a regular basis. Effort needs to be put in to ensure that the communication is relevant, warranted and timely, but when this is the case it becomes a very powerful tool.
Cons	It's now very easy to blast emails to half the world and just as easy to destroy potential relationships with full mailboxes and irrelevant, unwanted 'spam'. As with many technologies, such as the car, it can transform life or be a dangerous tool, depending on how it is used.
Success factors	It is essential to personalise email marketing if it is to be successful. This also means that it needs to be targeted to the recipient, with relevant messages, content and follow-on. That target might be a segment of one, as in one-to-one marketing, or more likely it may be a tightly defined group, but it must not cause the customer to ask 'Why am I getting this – is it for my benefit or yours?'

5 Creative suites

What are they?	A wide range of creative software suites are now available that allow non-professionals to design and implement all sorts of multimedia materials, including websites, sales and marketing materials and even DVDs. Tools such as Photoshop, and Dreamweaver from Adobe, or Expressions from Microsoft allow anyone to develop professional-looking materials for a variety of uses. This is not to say that you shouldn't be seeking professional support for the majority of marketing activities, but these tools can be used to produce highly professional and personalised materials for customer proposals and other one-to-one situations.
Pros	Powerful creative tools mean that marketing teams can easily create and customise a range of high-impact marketing collaterals. This is particularly useful when budgets are tight, because businesses can still deliver targeted sales presentations and proposals that add an extra touch to customer interactions.
Cons	They are generally more difficult to use effectively than simpler tools such as Microsoft PowerPoint, but then again you are getting a much more professional-looking result.
Success factors	Don't think these are an opportunity to take all creative work in-house. But do consider how you can use them selectively to deliver customised, impactful materials. Of course, if you have the time to learn and use these applications properly, and money is tight, you might wish to extend their use to wider material production.

6 Web 2.0 and social networking

What is it?	The second generation of the World Wide Web, Web 2.0, brings a new level of interactivity and connectedness. The phenomenal success of the likes of Facebook and MySpace provide new ways to communicate and engage with customers. Whether it is networks of potential customers or business audiences, the links between them give rise to the possibility of viral marketing, whereby you seed a message and it spreads like a virus around the world in a matter of hours. Examples can be seen every day on YouTube: some of these are put up by individuals but increasingly businesses are uploading promotional videos of adverts and new product launches as an integral part of campaigns.
Pros	Not only does viral marketing spread very quickly but when it is user- or customer-generated it has a bigger impact as a result of its independence. Of course, it is also very cost effective.

Cons	Negative messages propagate as quickly as positive ones. Another danger is of businesses being perceived as abusing or blatantly manipulating opinions and audiences. The backlash from this can seriously damage valuable, long-standing reputations.
Success factors	Try to harness the power of these networks. Seed useful and interesting information and ideas into key communities, and position the business at the forefront of your market. From celebrity chefs to large corporations, reputation and reputation management has become a critical success factor in modern business. Web 2.0 can act as a powerful tool to amplify that reputation, whether positive or negative. So pay attention to how communities perceive the business and investigate ways to harness the power of viral marketing.

7 Blogs

What are they?	A blog is an online journal, where the interactive nature of the web allows communities and audiences to comment on and link to the thoughts and views expressed. Topics cover the whole human life cycle, but many companies now publish blogs written by thought leaders in the business as a way to engage with customers and markets. Whether created on the internet or on the company intranet, blogs provide a place where groups of people with an interest in a topic can converge to share ideas and opinions.
Pros	Essentially a broadcast medium that links to external blog sites as well as the business's own website, a blog provides interested communities with an open forum for discussion. The technology behind these sites gives blogs a wide reach, making them a very efficient and effective way to disseminate messages. They can be a powerful tool to express thought leadership opinions, as well as acting as a focus for special interest groups. Of course, a blog is a two-way medium, so it can also provide you with valuable ideas, feedback and opinion.
Cons	Like the rest of the Web 2.0 phenomenon, negative or damaging opinions from disgruntled customers or even employees can be broadcast and spread around cyberspace at the touch of a button. While ranting will be seen as just that, in contrast coherent, well-argued opinions that conflict with the party line will need careful handling.
Success factors	Allow and encourage the business and key employees to become opinion leaders on the web by using blogs to engage with interested communities. Successful blogs are likely to be interesting, thought-provoking and often controversial. Consider how a blog can be used to interact with your target audiences and to address the issues that are important to them. Try to balance this with your own thoughts and opinions.

8 Project and portfolio management software

What is it?	Project management software applications are used to scope, plan, monitor and control the implementation of ideas and activities using project management techniques. They provide a structured approach to managing complex programmes and campaigns. Most major marketing initiatives can and should be viewed as projects and need to be planned as such – too many initiatives fail to deliver against anticipated benefits, often because they are poorly project managed.
Pros	Project management software provides a very effective way of planning project activities, making it clear what the objectives are and who does what when. Simple outputs can also provide a clear communication mechanism for all stakeholders. Web-based applications used across an organisation also provide a means for managing the portfolio of projects as a whole, as opposed to managing individual projects in isolation.
Cons	Most project management tools are too complex for marketing activity. They tend to focus on detailed task and resource management, as opposed to typical success factors such as having clear objectives, an effective stakeholder management process and simple risk management.
Success factors	Be clear about which activities can be implemented quickly – those that fall into the 'just do it' category – and which will benefit from project management techniques. Then find a simple and easy-to-use web-based software product and ensure that key people know how to use it. Finally, don't forget that project management is as much about the softer elements, including setting the vision, leading the team, negotiating with stakeholders and managing up, down and sideways, as it is about the technical aspects of plotting the critical path.

9 Workflow and document management

What is it?	The creative and production side of marketing generates a lot of material in the form of documents, concepts, proofs and so on. The related areas of workflow and document management can help to manage and audit the life cycles of these activities, automatically directing work and approvals to the next stage in the process and capturing every version of the document for archive purposes. Web content management systems are a related technology, required to manage the large amount of information and content on the business's various websites.

Pros	Such systems can ease the management and production cycle for large or complex marketing projects. They also provide a repository for all marketing materials throughout the development cycle, so that ideas and themes can be revisited easily, whether or not they actually made it to production. Finally, they also provide version management and control, which helps marketing teams manage everything from presentation variants to marketing plans to collateral copy.
Cons	There are very few disadvantages apart from the cost. Remember that developing and adhering to a defined process is not always needed unless you have a lot of large, complex projects.
Success factors	Consider these systems for large marketing teams regularly producing a lot of marketing materials, including ads, mailers, sales collateral, case studies, web content and the like. The cost over and above a shared file system and email is only really justified for big teams and high-production volumes.

10 Business intelligence (BI)

What is it?	A set of information analysis tools to provide support for business and marketing decision making. Business intelligence solutions take data input from databases linked to CRM, other operational systems and even external systems. Such systems relate to and provide support for performance management: capturing trends and enabling 'what if?' analysis on business drivers and KPIs. Business intelligence should be used to help managers filter and make sense of the deluge of data available, so that they can better understand trends and opportunities. Information is often presented to the user through a 'dashboard'.
Pros	BI can be a powerful tool for marketing teams to assess performance and explore options for such things as pricing and promotional offers.
Cons	As with many data-driven systems, although they can support 'what if?' analysis, they primarily tell you what has been happening. So the indicators are therefore lagging the current environment. No one in their right mind would drive a car by looking in the rear-view mirror, so users must be wary of this notion when driving the business.

Success factors	A marketing team that invests in understanding the external and internal drivers and environmental trends will benefit from such systems. But BI systems can sometimes seem to promise the world. As with CRM, it is often best to start with a small pragmatic BI solution that really distils the essence of the business. For most small businesses this starts with a spreadsheet or simple database tools that can be used for 'what if?' analysis. If required, more sophisticated systems can then be put in place, depending on the complexity.

How do I keep balance?

Before going out and investing in the latest and greatest, remember that technology is just an enabler. Success will ultimately depend on your ability to lead people, your behaviours and how you interact with others.

Be wary of being drawn into the cutting edge too quickly, but equally be prepared to take the initiative to get a step ahead if you see a technology-driven breakthrough opportunity that will transform your marketing activity. Finally, if you do decide to introduce new systems to your team, think carefully about the possible risks – what could go wrong?

STOP – THINK – ACT

You may already have been aware of many of these modern technologies, but you should now understand how each can be used to support the adoption of a consistent and effective approach to marketing based on the best practices identified in Chapter 3. Use technology selectively to impact on performance in ways that minimise complexity, bureaucracy and cost.

Reflect on each of the technologies presented and ask yourself and the team these questions:

What should we do?	What technologies are available that will help to improve effectiveness and efficiency?
Who do we need to involve?	Who would benefit and why?
What resources will we require?	What level of investment would be required?
What is the timing?	When would be a good time to introduce the new technology – is there a 'window of opportunity'?

Visit **www.Fast-Track-Me.com** to use the Fast Track online planning tool.

Mobile marketing – an up-close and interactive way to market

Cigdem Gogus

Basically, mobile marketing is the use of a mobile network as the delivery channel by a well-identified promoter for the impersonal presentation and promotion of goods, services and ideas. It involves the distribution of messages valued by the consumer, while at the same time it seeks to enhance revenue for the firm. Although quite a recent phenomenon, the mobile marketing industry has grown rapidly – for example, growing from £2 billion to £8 billion between 2003 and 2005, and reaching over 500 million users worldwide.

The mobile channel is able to deliver a higher level of interactivity, timeliness, personalisation and context sensitivity than any other marketing channel. Companies are increasingly using mobile marketing, integrating this new channel into their business operations as a tool to foster and maintain strong relationships with their customers.

Most mobile marketing campaigns include one or a combination of the following elements: mobile internet banner ads; sponsored awareness/information messages; advertising messages; promotion alerts; coupons and promotional offerings; text-to-win competitions/quizzes; loyalty point systems; and free content (e.g. logos, ringtones and games). Current mobile marketing activities, in the main, are centred on advertising and sales promotions aimed at consumers. But there is still some confusion around terminology regarding the three related concepts – mobile marketing, advertising and sales promotions – which are sometimes used interchangeably by consumers, firms and researchers. The flexibility afforded by the mobile platform adds to the blurring of distinctions between different types of marketing message. This makes it difficult to determine the different responses that consumers will exhibit for different marketing messages (e.g. sales promotions versus advertising).

For mobile marketing to reach its full potential of personalised information available anytime, any place, it is necessary to understand the unique aspects of the mobile medium. An individual's willingness to respond to a mobile marketing message is likely to be influenced by their location, time of the day, week of the year and so on. Individuals may have a routine that takes them to certain places at certain times that may have relevance for mobile marketing. If so, marketers can pinpoint locations and attempt to provide content at the right time. For example, consider an office worker who lets her mobile network operator know that she would like to receive information during weekdays, from 12.30 to 1 pm, about the special offers from local sandwich bars within a quarter-mile radius of her office. The consumer would regard this type of information as valuable, resulting in a win–win situation for all parties involved. Similar ways of personalisation of content are possible by capturing and analysing customer data, as well as identifying information that customers would find valuable and beneficial. The ultimate goal of the marketing communication should be to make the customer feel understood and to establish a one-to-one personal relationship.

As mobile marketing has a more invasive nature than all other media, respect for consumer privacy lies at the heart of building and maintaining trust, as well as providing a pleasant experience to users. There is evidence that customers don't want to be contacted unless they explicitly state otherwise, so in permission-based marketing the customer is approached to ask for their permission to be sent different types of communication in a personal way. In addition, the information received must be of high value to gain the user's permission. For example, consider that you are soon to take a flight and you receive a sponsored message saying that your flight is delayed by eight hours. This results in you avoiding a long wait in the airport lounge. This type of communication encourages consumers to participate in interactive marketing campaigns because they are rewarded in some way for attention to increasingly relevant messages.

The idea of a message being sent directly to an individual's phone also has legislative implications. For example, within the EU, privacy and consumer rights issues led to establishing opt-in schemes. In essence, opt-in schemes involve the user in agreeing to receive mobile marketing communications before anything is sent. Several current initiatives and industry groups, such as the Mobile Data Association,[1] are spearheading the building of standards of best practice for the mobile data industry. The aim is to establish easy and clear guidelines and practices to enable consumers to opt in and opt out as they wish.

Mobile marketing offers many opportunities, but care needs to be taken. Many consumers are likely to be put off by too much unwanted information over the mobile network to the detriment of both the promoter and the operator. So a good understanding of the principles and then their sensible application can increase the possibilities for success.

---

[1] www.themda.org.

5

IMPLEMENTING CHANGE

There is no single right approach for sustainable success in marketing. You will need to decide for yourself what is and is not appropriate for your team and business. In the previous chapters we have looked at a marketing framework (Chapter 3) and the top ten technologies (Chapter 4) available to support the marketing effort. So now is the time to decide how to apply those ideas to your environment to really make it happen. You will doubtless want to do a few things differently, so think ahead and plan the implementation of change carefully.

Planning the way ahead

By now you probably have some idea of how your marketing framework should look and which elements form the key building blocks of your team approach. If the gaps are still unclear, or if you are seeking to make your business 'world class', then consider undertaking a structured audit based on the integrated marketing framework (see page 177 in the Director's Toolkit).

As the framework suggests, before plunging into planning changes, it's best to understand where you are, where you want to go and what the options are for getting there. Perhaps you might want to have some brainstorming meetings with the marketing team, and perhaps even with senior management stakeholders, to look at each of the key elements of the marketing framework and identify the areas of relative strength and weakness. These meetings are sure to generate lots of ideas for change. But you can't do everything at once, so identify the key areas to focus on.

The following example may be wider than you need or can handle at the moment, but it illustrates what happens when you tackle the whole topic of an integrated marketing framework. Imagine that these brainstorming meetings have identified the following aspects of your marketing framework, which your team feels represent the greatest opportunities for improvement.

→ **The marketing planning process appears somewhat disjointed and perhaps divorced from the focus of the business.** While there is an overall strategy in place, it does not put into words the current business imperatives that should guide the medium-term marketing thinking. Specifically, it is unclear what the priorities are in terms of high-growth and high-emphasis product markets, and where the greatest threats may come from. As a result, there may be a lack of alignment between marketing direction and business objectives. Perhaps the team needs to strengthen this area, allocate more resources into the understanding and development phases where this thinking and planning takes place, and start using programme gates to sign off strategy and planning activities.

→ **Everyone appears to know who the major competitors are but no one really knows much about them.** What is their product-market focus, how do they differentiate themselves, how are they positioning themselves and what are their future strategies likely to be? This knowledge is critical in planning your product and market strategies. Without it, you may have no idea of how to challenge or react to changes in the competitive environment. Perhaps a quarterly or half-yearly structured review and analysis of major competitors and potential substitutes would provide a useful impetus for marketing planning.

→ **Both these realisations point to a lack of evidence or data-based decision making.** Assumptions and gut feel will always be an element of decision making, but marketing teams often need greater clarity in terms of how these are balanced with facts and evidence. The team should consider strengthening systems and processes to support a greater proportion of evidence-based decisions and also to monitor the ongoing status of assumptions when these are needed.

→ **Because of the constant pressure on marketing teams, just like the rest of the business, there is a tendency to deliver a marketing programme and to move on.** It is a common trait in business: salespeople often used to get the order and move on to the next opportunity. But marketing teams should recognise the benefits of reviewing programmes and activities in order to close them after delivery. This means that teams can learn and capture what has worked well and what not so well, in order to help select more effective strategies and deliver more efficient programmes in the future. Consider implementing a semi-formal review to close each significant project or programme activity.

→ **The team feels that the breadth and choice of marketing programmes has become somewhat staid and one dimensional.** Programmes have centred on a relatively small selection of activities, such as exhibition events, advertising and sales promotions, to revitalise mid-life products. Perhaps it's now time to step up a gear and identify a more powerful selection of programmes to support a leading market position, develop key relationships and drive revenue. Maybe in future the team should consider more engaging and encompassing activities, such as customer advocacy and nurture programmes, sponsorship or a variety of public relations programmes, to achieve objectives with more zest and variety.

→ **Customer interactions are not well coordinated.** Groups including sales, customer support and even different teams within marketing are all communicating daily with customers via email, telephone and face to face. Messages and timing are driven without reference to each other and responses are captured in disparate systems. A customer relationship management (CRM) system would help to coordinate all these dialogues, providing consistency, a better customer experience and vastly improved internal efficiency.

→ **There seems to be an issue with internal marketing.** Most activities tend to be focused externally in order to generate revenues and market share. However, employees, particularly sales and customer-facing teams, are key stakeholder audiences who need to be nurtured and engaged. Whether through tools such as emails and the company intranet, or engagement programmes such as workshops or including employees in sponsorships, it's important to communicate the business's proposition and activity to these teams to get leverage and ensure that customers and markets get a consistent message. Consider implementing these sorts of technologies and programmes to keep everyone motivated and on the same page.

So already you have some great ideas for improvement, but how do you start to implement them? Clearly some of these changes are significant and it would therefore be unwise to 'just do it'. But at the same time you need to get on and make progress, so these ideas might provide an opportunity to make an impression. It is vital that implementing these changes goes well.

QUICK TIP *BE SENSITIVE TO CULTURE*
While some of us will want to take the bull by the horns and implement many of these changes on a 'just do it' basis, you also need to be aware of the culture within the organisation. The 'just do it' approach works well in a culture where good ideas and actions are encouraged and 'to ask permission is to seek denial'. However, more consensus-driven cultures might need wider buy-in from various stakeholders before you set off on your crusade.

How should we introduce changes?

One thing that is certain is that a number of people will have to accept changes in the way they currently do their jobs. Such change creates opportunity for some but can be painful for others. You have started the change process strongly by including your team in the early identification of the need for change. But you also need to make sure you take all stakeholders along with you from the start of the journey.

Make a complete list of these stakeholders. First, get the buy-in of the more senior members on the list – those that are part of your team as well as senior management from other parts of the business. To get their support, explain the business drivers for the change and the benefits that you are expecting to accrue. Next, deal with the other stakeholders by using the agreement of the senior people as reference to spur buy-in from these other players. You don't necessarily need to arrange specific meetings, but could include such discussions as part of regular meetings. The trick is to engage early and start from the perspective of the benefits for the greater good. There will always be individual agendas, but it will be very difficult for anyone to combat this broad viewpoint.

 CASE STORY **NOKIA CORPORATION, MARK'S STORY**

Narrator Mark is the UK communications director, responsible for all marketing messaging into the UK market.

Context Nokia is a world leader in mobility, driving the transformation and growth of the converging internet and communications industries. The company makes a wide range of mobile devices and, through these products, provides people with experiences in music, navigation, video, television, imaging, games and business mobility. To remain a market leader, good change management is essential.

Issue Mark noticed that many managers formed teams by either choosing people they liked or they thought could work together. They would then invest in various team-building days, management meetings, mode of operation studies and so on, to attempt to create focused groups. Unfortunately, it appeared to Mark that the more talented the individuals, the less able they were to work together or with other areas of the business.

Solution Mark realised that, like many successful companies, Nokia had attracted a number of new staff, many of whom were not familiar with the Nokia values. He was also aware that to the Nokia staff these new managers would often appear brash and threatening. As a result, Mark decided that building new teams would be far easier if there was a clear set of goals from the company board. So, as he took on each team member, he briefed them on their main task and focus, setting deadlines and prime objectives. At no stage until the team was complete and had achieved the first stages of planning did Mark allow them to all meet officially.

Learning By maintaining distance between team members until tasks are assigned, you can avoid the group splitting into factions. More importantly, the team members do not have the opportunity to decide who they do and do not like before they have seen what each member and their staff can achieve. The greatest advantage in Mark's approach is that the team's focus remains on the board's wishes and not on avoidance and argument. This is a powerful way of working that is especially good over large geographical distances or for managing teams with diverse tasks.

You also need to work out what your objectives are from the change pro- gramme. Decide how you will know when you have succeeded in creating a more sustainable approach to marketing, and give yourself a realistic but flexible time target to get there. Make sure the objectives indicate the clear boundaries that you will operate within, to avoid the possibility of 'scope creep', which is an inherent risk with such funda- mental organisational change. For example, suppose you're trying to get the company's strategy clearly articulated in order to ensure closer mar- keting alignment. Scope creep would mean that you start to do the articulating yourself, risking treading on toes, duplicating effort and even getting it wrong. Your objective is to get the people responsible to articu- late the strategy.

So you now have a clear understanding of where you want to go and how you want to get there, and you've got the buy-in of key stakeholders for the journey ahead. As with the marketing process itself, you can develop a plan of action for the change with a list of activities, responsi- bilities and timelines. Here's a simple example based on some of the topics at the start of this chapter. This does not go into detailed work breakdowns or even project aims and objectives, but instead highlights how change projects within marketing might be initiated.

Phase 1 Marketing process

    Activity 1.1 Develop: implement a new stage as part of the develop phase to ensure that strategies and plans align and match with business imperatives and activity

Activity 1.2 Understand: Implement a regular competitive analysis every three or six months as part of ongoing marketing understanding

Activity 1.3 Review: Implement a semi-formal review to close every project and programme, capturing learning experiences to improve effectiveness and efficiency

Phase 2 CRM

Activity 2.1 Understand how customer data is currently captured, manipulated and used by various groups within the business

Activity 2.2 Initiate a project to define a business case for the implementation of a CRM system to consolidate and coordinate all customer interactions

Phase 3 Internal marketing

Activity 3.1 Develop internal marketing programmes to communicate with employee audiences through both push and pull technologies, as well as engagement through external-facing programmes such as sponsorships

Each of these activities will have a start and completion date, as well as an owner responsible for driving the project through to closure. Depending on the size of the change implementation, you might choose to set milestones to review performance and progress and check that the programme is still aligned.

It may be that some elements of the framework are small enough to be implemented by informal meetings or as part of everyday operations. Implementation planning can be very useful, but some activities are straightforward enough just to get on with. Others, such as the CRM project, might require the development of a full business case to justify the time and money of developing new technology and processes. If the change project is not straightforward then consider entering these activities into a Gantt chart, like the one overleaf, so that it is easy for everyone to see timelines, dependencies and deadlines. This doesn't need to be in a project management tool, but if you're using one then it should generate this for you automatically from your list of tasks.

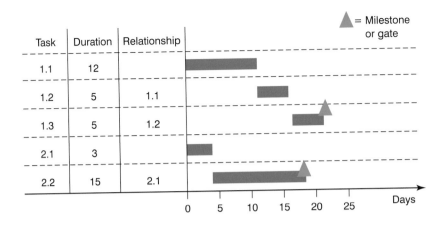

Now you have an outline plan of how to implement the marketing frame-work, whether that is company-wide, across a division or just for your team. Another critically important aspect of implementing change – whatever the scale – is to communicate the key elements of the plan and map the progress against it. This brings the change to life, keeping it visible and reinforcing the fact that it is a reality and is happening. Whether you communicate via email, newsletters or face to face through meetings or lunchtime briefings will depend on the complexity of the change project and the size and location of the stakeholder audience. Use whatever communication tools are appropriate to ensure that these stakeholders are kept informed and remain supportive of the programme.

If it is a significant change programme, part of this communication (as well as a powerful management tool) is a regular report that sum-marises the status of the project. This should capture the essence of the plan and the progress to date, as well as a risk analysis covering poten-tial obstacles and contingencies. You should highlight what is working well and what has gone wrong. Of course, if you're using an appropriate project and programme management tool to support the rollout of mar-keting activities, it's likely that this could also be used to support the rollout of the change programme and to deliver this report for you.

Don't forget that you will need budget and resources to deliver this change programme: don't be tempted just to squeeze it into the sched-ule. Work out what ideally you will need, remembering that you will have to justify expenses and resources. This is a mini business case, putting forward a reasoned, cost-justified argument for investment. So it's probably not sufficient to say, for example, that without the change pro-gramme the organisation will die. You need more specifics. Look for success stories of companies who have strengthened their marketing capabilities, process and systems. Point to things that have gone wrong in the past and how much they have cost the company. Look for 'quick wins' – simple things you can do before you get your new budget or things that you can do quickly afterwards. Make the quick wins as con-crete in financial terms as you possibly can.

QUICK TIP 'INVESTMENT' PORTFOLIO

Just as you will need budget and resources to change and improve marketing processes and activity, you will also need time, which is among the scarcest of resources. Consciously determine how much of your resource pot – whether money, time or people – you want to invest in the change programme. Every portfolio should include some investment or speculation activity, but decide on the balance between that and the day-to-day activity that you need to deliver against.

A simple quick win could be the suggestion that you add in to the sales process a win/loss analysis. Even an hour spent with the salesperson and their manager could find an insight that will improve their win/loss ratio and feed back into the marketing process. Conversations triggered by questions like 'Why did the customer really buy?' or 'What went wrong?' can affect anything from product features to marketing messages.

Ensuring success – keeping the plan on track

What approach should we use?

Now you have to keep the project plan on track. Simply putting a plan together does not mean it will happen. The keywords are action and implementation. Think about the three Ps that you will need to manage:

plan (tasks and timings), **people** (keeping stakeholders motivated and on track) and **performance** (the project objectives). Keep your focus equally on all three.

The plan-do-check-act (PDCA) cycle (see figure) is a widely used continuous improvement approach to managing a project or team.

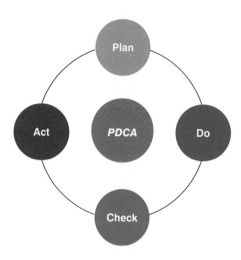

→ **Plan.** You have to plan your activities, as discussed above, perhaps including a Gantt chart so that the actions and deadlines are easily visible.

→ **Do.** As you might guess, this means getting on with and completing the activities identified in the plan.

→ **Check.** This is where it gets iterative. Stop and check the progress you're making towards implementing the plan. A simple analogy is to think of swimming front crawl in the sea as opposed to in a pool with lines on the bottom. Most people need to stop every 25 yards or so to check that they are not swimming in a big circle! A regular check will reveal any problems with the delivery of the plan, the people and resources you are engaging, or the performance and results being delivered.

→ **Act.** Make decisions and take action to bring the project back on track by resolving the problems.

In summary:

P – plan ahead

D – do what we say we are going to do

C – check performance

A – act to bring performance back on track.

What routines should we set up?

Regular structured communication, with the implied defined tasks and milestones, is the key to keeping things on track, so it's important to get into some good routines. Complex situations can be dramatically simplified through regular review meetings. Face-to-face meetings are the best way, although distance might sometimes mean that you need to take the second-best option of a video conference or even a phone call. Depending on what you are looking to achieve, these reviews may be a quick and simple five-minute call or coffee-break update, through to a full-day workshop involving all key stakeholders.

How do we stay flexible?

While you need to understand the principles of planning and performance monitoring, you also need to remain flexible and responsive to the team and how things are going. Think about how tight or loose your controls really need to be. Too loose and you run the risk of missing deadlines or going off at a tangent, but too tight and you run the risk of reducing the team's motivation and losing key stakeholders' commitment.

This balance is key to good leadership. Getting too caught up with either the process or the technologies that you're using for support can sap energy – both your own and that of your team, stifling creativity and motivation and reducing inputs to a mechanical level. Processes and technologies such as project management or CRM are there to support the achievement of your end goals in the most effective and efficient manner. They are a means to an end, not an end in themselves, so don't let them distract or get in the way of getting the job done. There are too many examples of managers becoming so intent with ticking the boxes on a project or process that the team around them ignores shortcuts and better ways of doing things so as not to rock the boat.

> QUICK TIP **FOCUS ON THE GOAL**
> Things change, possibly even to the extent that the goal needs to change. Be prepared for this eventuality and don't expect the situation at the end to be as it was when you started. So, while you focus day to day on delivering activities on the critical path, bear in mind that it is quite possible that you might need to adjust the strategy to accommodate a change in the external environment or when you spot a divergence from your desired path. Keep calm, think of the best way forward from where you are and develop a skill for recognising how far to roll back the plan when a change of course is needed.

Hopefully you will also have a balance within the team of rational thinkers and those with creative talents. You will spot the people who will help more on one side of the rational/creative spectrum, and learn to rely on the rational ones to keep the project steady and the creative ones from time to time to take a huge step forward. The best teams have a powerful combination of each kind of talent – harnessing innovation, creativity and experimentation but supporting this by clear and rational dependability. Some people go from one mountain top to the next by plodding down the mountainside then plodding up the other one. Others prefer to take a run and a leap and hope they make it: the rational thinkers might suggest they strap on a parachute pack before they leap. When they do make it, they have made a great contribution to the team; when they fail, you and the team will have to help them recover. It's the balance of the two that ensures not only success but also the best result possible.

Critical success factors

So how can we increase our chances of success?

As you start to implement your marketing framework, consider the factors that will drive success for you, your team and the business. You can't focus on everything at once, so where do you start?

While the integrated marketing framework is comprehensive, it is not necessarily difficult to implement. However, it is clear that not all factors are equally important, and success appears to come down to getting the following factors right.

→ Focus on opportunities of high value that fit with current business priorities – this tends to get everyone's attention and commitment.

→ Ensure that senior management (right up to the CEO) shows *active* commitment to marketing as a key business driver and differentiator – after all, it is these people who will have the greatest impact on business culture, so if they don't take it seriously then no one else will.

→ Install systems and tools to support the consistent application of best practices across all teams, creating a common language for marketing excellence.

→ Develop project management skills to improve overall effectiveness and efficiency, as well as the quality of the team deliverables.

→ Reward people for sharing ideas and knowledge, in non-financial ways as well as through bonuses.

→ Finally, communicate successes or quick wins to all interested stakeholders so that people can see that the overall approach is working and worthwhile.

STOP – THINK – ACT

After reading this chapter you will be aware that implementing a comprehensive approach to marketing is not necessarily quick or easy. It needs to be planned and implemented using a disciplined approach. Use the team audit in Chapter 2 to identify the gaps in your current approach. (Note that there is a more comprehensive team audit in the Director's Toolkit on page 171.) Then identify the actions you will need to take to make your approach succeed.

What should we do?	What stages and tasks are appropriate?
Who do we need to involve?	Who needs to be involved and why?
What resources will we require?	What information, facilities, materials, equipment or budget will be required?
What is the timing?	How long will each activity typically take?

Visit **www.Fast-Track-Me.com** to use the Fast Track online planning tool.

EXPERT VOICE

New product development – paying attention to critical decisions

Professor David Birchall

Innovation is seen as the 'life blood' of organisations. Without it, businesses become tired and eventually wither away. The marketing function has a key role to play in innovation, which can come through new product development, enhancements to existing products, new or improved business processes or the development of new markets. In addition, many organisations are developing their brand by emphasising their innovative capability in providing solutions to client problems. So marketing has a role to play in identifying markets and understanding market conditions, preparing markets for the product launch and identifying new approaches to take products and services to market. But many organisations are now seeing the importance of engaging the marketing function throughout all stages of new product development (NPD). Why is this?

NPD has become increasingly complex and, for it to be a success, those involved in its management need to be highly focused on achieving the end product but also aware and sensitive to the wider changes in their business environment and their likely impact. They need to pay particular attention to those decisions that can really make a difference to success in their own particular context, and concentrate effort on effective implementation. Many businesses now see NPD as a process rather than as a discrete element such as R&D and prototyping, and they are seeing it as a cross-disciplinary activity where many functions, including marketing, have a key role to play throughout the process. But additionally those involved in marketing possess many of the skills needed to face up to the challenge of bringing new ideas to market in the changing business environment – and could play an even greater role.

The management of NPD is an important element in innovation success. Research done by Robert Cooper at McMaster University over many years has examined best practice NPD and, in particular, a stage-gate process involving clear decision points on the route.[1] So why, when the features making up best practice are recognised, do organisations not achieve greater success? A recent study in the UK reported that organisations have not been particularly successful in adopting best practices.[2] These researchers conclude that this results from an inability in execution due to poor management practices, including poor management of change and the inadequacy of training, insufficient investment in capital assets and R&D, and an inadequate collaborative infrastructure external to the enterprise to get the necessary support for those within the enterprise. Another reason is undoubtedly inherent in the process. Overcoming stage gates is often seen as the result of an objective evaluation of a project. But no organisational evaluation is free of politicking. Project champions are essential in the support of initiatives, but when the project champion loses objectivity then stage-gate decisions are often seen as subject to influence, with approval often granted at the expense of other more worthy initiatives that have a less influential champion. The marketing department has a role to play in bringing analytical skills, an external perspective and an unbiased view to this process.

An important role for senior management during the innovation process, often not given sufficient emphasis, is constantly ensuring that those involved in the day-to-day activity don't lose sight of the overall strategic objective. The marketing function, because of its outward focus, can have a major role to play here. Also, senior managers need to ensure a balance between the needs of one project and those of the portfolio overall. Communication of decisions impacts on staff attitudes, as does non-communication. So communicating strategic fit, the rationale for decisions and the recognition of implications are all important for staff motivation and commitment, and help to overcome the many hurdles encountered in the innovation process, whether new products, approaches to market or processes.

Many argue that the innovation process should be treated as a project. But all too often project management fails to deliver on time, due to ineffective decision making. Staff involved in projects often report too much

[1] Cooper, R.G. (2008), 'Perspective: the stage-gate idea-to-launch process – update, what's new, and nexgen systems', *Journal of Product Innovation Management*, 25(3), 213–32.
[2] AIM (2005), *Making Best Practice Stick: How UK Firms Can Increase Productivity by Adopting Leading-Edge Working Practies*, London: Advanced Institute of Management Research.

bureaucracy, built-in delays arising from the need for decisions from other business areas and, in many cases, a lack of understanding of the detailed needs by the decision makers. So how can one ensure that decision-making authority is at the appropriate level in the organisation?

This management of a portfolio of innovation projects involves, at times, tough decisions relating to specific projects. Individual projects may well be on track to achieve the stated goals at the outset, but may no longer fit the strategic demands being placed on the portfolio. The external perspectives brought by the marketing function can help project leaders keep abreast of whether or not specific projects are in alignment with external changes. The price of termination may seem high for those individuals committed to the particular project, and project leaders may need to exercise high-level skills to rebuild the personal and team motivation of those left disappointed. Additionally, in this work set-up, for the project manager a focus solely on achieving narrow project targets is no longer sufficient. Project managers now need to be much more aware of the strategic direction of the business and the dynamics of the portfolio. They need to be applying skills in managing 'upwards' and 'sideways', to ensure that their own project does not fall off the radar screen and is clearly seen to be in line with business needs, and that adequate resources remain available to enable project execution. This requires greater sensitivity to external events, using good external networks and relationship and influencing skills – something marketing professionals can often assist with.

In many organisations there is considerable pressure to condense the time to market following initial project approval. This is leading to a rethink about the innovation process. Radically different approaches may be called for to fast track development. This may well involve more concurrent working and overlapping of activities that were traditionally performed in sequence. The time imperative may justify some duplication of efforts and the resultant greater costs to secure market position and high returns.

Over time, processes are embedded in organisations and become inflexible. They get out of alignment with organisational needs. While regular review can lead to improvement, this will only occur if decision making about processes is clear and all stakeholders are engaged to ensure improvements happen. 'Learning before', 'learning during' and 'learning after' (described by Chris Collison and Geoff Parcell in their book *Learning to Fly*[3]) is an approach to accelerate performance improvement by ongoing sharing of knowledge, insights and emerging good practice. Prior to project approval, sponsors are required to demonstrate how learning from previous projects has influenced the proposal; how involvement of knowledgeable

[3] Collison, C. and Parcell, G. (2004), *Learning To Fly: Practical Lessons from One of the World's Leading Knowledge Companies*, Oxford: Capstone.

peers during project meetings introduces new thinking during execution; and how project review supports the transfer of learning to other projects. Key to the ongoing success of the enterprise is the issue of capability. But capability building is no longer confined by the boundaries of the enterprise. Key to future innovation success is the capability located within the supply network. This capability includes the ability to work effectively in a dynamic network, so as to achieve new products and services fit for market.

EXPERT VOICE

CAREER
FAST TRACK

Whatever you have decided to do in terms of developing your career as a manager, to be successful you need to take control, plan ahead and focus on the things that will really make a difference.

The first ten weeks of a new role will be critical. Get them right and you will be off to a flying start and will probably succeed. Get them wrong and you will come under pressure and even risk being moved on rather quickly. Plan this initial period to make sure you are not overwhelmed by the inevitable mass of detail that will assail you on arrival. Make sure that other people's priorities do not put you off the course that you have set yourself.

Once you have successfully eased yourself into your new role and gained the trust of your boss and the team, you can start to make things happen. First, focus on your leadership style and how it needs to change to suit the new role; then focus on the team. Are they the right people and, if so, what will make them work more effectively as a marketing team?

Finally, at the appropriate time, you need to think about your next career move, and whether you are interested in getting to the top by becoming a company director. This is not for everyone, as the commitment, time and associated stress can be offputting, but the sense of responsibility and leadership can be enormously rewarding.

You've concentrated on performance up until now – now it's time to look at your Fast Track career.

THE FIRST TEN WEEKS

The first ten weeks of starting a new role as the leader of a marketing team are probably the most critical – get them wrong and you risk failure, get them right and you will enjoy and thrive in your new role. What do you need to do, where should you focus and what must you avoid at all costs?

To ensure they start off on the right foot and build a solid foundation for themselves, Fast Track managers will seek to understand key facts, build relationships and develop simple mechanisms for monitoring and control – establishing simple but effective team processes. Again, these tasks will be simplified using modern technologies and so will become effortless and part of day-to-day behaviour.

Changing roles

Why is this a critical time?

We have repeatedly said that marketing affects everyone in the business and that everyone in the business needs to be involved with the marketing function. This means that the arrival of a new manager with a marketing tag will be scrutinised and, frankly, criticised by the whole organisation. Their first impression has to be that you are going to listen to them, react to their problems and not pretend to have the solution to all the organisation's difficulties.

People don't necessarily need to see instant answers, but they will expect you to bring some of your own views and ideas to the role. You will want to put in place a process that will focus marketing effort, get the general direction right and then assist people to implement the strategy efficiently. On the other hand, you need to make sure that people recognise that once a marketing decision is taken everyone is expected to work within it. So, in summary, don't go off at half-cock but show that there is value in people accepting a well thought-out and discussed marketing strategy.

Remember the expression that you only have one chance to make a good first impression. You have a clean slate, so use it well. Make a strong start in the first few months and you will have quickly established yourself as someone who brings value to the marketing team and the business. Get it wrong and it could impact your reputation and relationships with others in the business for a long time. Hopefully you will be joining an environment with few preconceptions. Take advantage of this and also your fresh perspective on the situation. Don't try to change everything as soon as you get there, but be prepared to offer an external perspective or to question the status quo. When consultants are called in to address a business issue they often say exactly the same things as some of the internal managers, but as outsiders their views are respected and acted upon. You could have the same influence in the early days. But be careful to frame your comments in a constructive manner in order to encourage the old timers to move with you. As you take on a new role your levels of energy and enthusiasm will be high, so use this and your time effectively to gain an early advantage and establish your credibility.

What are the potential pitfalls?

While this period of transition presents opportunities to make a good impression, take care not to get it wrong. It is difficult to recover from a bad start in a new role, particularly in a new organisation. Recognise that you will be faced with a number of challenges to overcome.

→ You might lack knowledge and expertise in your new role, which could make you vulnerable to getting decisions wrong.

→ If you are new to the business you will most probably lack an understanding of the subtleties of the organisation and how things are done. This is a double-edged sword: it can put you at a disadvantage by not knowing certain processes or procedures, but equally it gives you a chance to question whether these ways of doing things are valid or just habit.

→ In every team there will be a mixture of people and politics – getting in with the wrong people can limit your opportunities for future promotion.

→ There will be a lot to do in a short period of time and you may well feel overwhelmed by it all.

→ Many effective managers rely heavily on their informal networks, but in the early stages of a new job in a new business these don't exist.

These pointers are true in any job but especially true in marketing. The problem is that at first you do not have the credibility to affect how people go about presenting the products to the market. Gain that credibility before you start advising people how to go about their jobs because it will not be possible later.

What is the worst-case scenario?

Because people might give the benefit of the doubt to those who are starting a new job or joining a new team, things often go well for a period of time. If you make mistakes they will forgive you because you're new to the job. This is referred to as the 'honeymoon period'. However, after a period of time (the first ten weeks), you will need to perform well and meet the expectations of key stakeholders. During the honeymoon period you will be cut some slack and you can use that either to weigh things up and get your first actions right or, of course, to hang yourself.

During this initial period, it is vital that you take the steps necessary to set yourself up for longer-term success. You don't want to make a good start but then have your efforts viewed as just another management initiative. Plan your first ten weeks carefully to ensure success over the short and long terms.

The first ten weeks

What should I do before I start?

Well, you're on the right track by reading this book! But you should also develop a to-do list of things you want to learn about, impact or prepare for. You probably did some research on the business and the market in order to get the job, but make sure you have as much information as possible at your fingertips. From marketing knowledge to details on the business and the industry, it will all stand you in good stead.

Think also about how you yourself will need to change. How will you behave differently, what knowledge will you need to gain and what new skills would be useful? Understanding these things will help to build your confidence.

What do the first ten weeks look like?

I like to follow the old flying adage of ANC – aviate, navigate and communicate – or the first aid ABC of airways, breathing and circulation. Whichever one appeals to you, the principle is to get the critical things done first. Get the aircraft under control, flying straight and level, with all the dials in the green. Work out where you are, where you are heading and how much fuel you have. When you are comfortable with that, you can start telling interested parties where you are and where you're planning to go.

You might be in a position to meet and discuss the role with the previous incumbent, to get their perspective as you start to build your picture of your route forward, but this is not always possible. Regardless of this, you can use the following suggestions to put together a plan for your first ten weeks in your new position in marketing.

Week 1: Meet and understand your customers

By this I mean your paying customers, out there in the marketplace. The important thing is to do this first, before you get embroiled in internal perspectives. It's also good to talk to them at this early stage because they will probably recognise that they are helping your 'education' and so are more likely to give you a complete picture of the situation.

Find out how customers view your offering: why they buy, what they like and don't like, and what they would say to other customers. Don't be tempted just to speak to strong advocates. Get the perspective of some less supportive customers as well. Try to extract the emotional dimensions as well as the hard, value-driven facts of the purchase decision and of living with that decision.

QUICK TIP *SEEK OUT DIFFERENT PERSPECTIVES*

Once you have a grasp of the business, try to go out with one of the sales team on a customer visit or perhaps an 'escalation meeting' to solve an issue. Understand the customer issues and observe how the company handles the situation and the customer reaction. In a consumer environment, you might just need to visit the customer service contact centre and listen to the calls and how they are handled, or spend some time in customer complaints. This kind of observation would be very instructive for many marketing and senior company executives to do on a regular basis.

You need to avoid making commitments at this stage, apart from that of having an ongoing dialogue. These are exploratory meetings to understand the customer perspective, not to address specific issues that inevitably arise or to discuss your plans. Let them know that it's your first week and that you wanted to get their input as the top priority. Obviously, as you talk to more customers, keep an eye out for developing trends, because whether these are issues or future requirements you will need to factor them in as part of your vision and plan.

Week 2: Understand where you are

Going back to the flying analogy, understanding where you are personally is like knowing what type of aircraft you are flying!

You obviously need to understand the business you are working in and the basis on which the company competes in the market. Assess the current situation in terms of where you think the business is and what point it has arrived at in its evolution. Is it a new or start-up business, or a steady-state organisation in a mature market? It might be in the process of rapid growth, or perhaps a business turnaround striving to regain profitability, or possibly even in a wind-down phase. This situation will be an important guide as you start to pull your thoughts and ideas together.

You will need to go beyond a superficial knowledge of the company's products and markets. You should either create or ensure you fully understand the product market matrix that defines the breakdown of exactly what the company offers to which customer markets. This powerful strategic tool also identifies the high and low emphasis segments: some will target growth, while some focus on opportunistic competition; others will aim to maintain the status quo, while others will be divested over time. Diagrammatically it looks like this:

	MARKET A	MARKET B	MARKET C
Product set 1	H>L	M>L	L>H
Product set 2	M>H	0>M	0>M

The first letter in each box shows the current strategic emphasis and the second letter the future strategic emphasis:

H = High level of activity using many resources

M = Medium level of activity

L = Low level of activity

0 = No activity at all

> = Change of emphasis from now into the future

You can see in this instance that the company plans to put a major emphasis on product set 2, taking it into two totally new markets and growing the importance of market A. At the same time product set 1 will be focused on the opportunities in market C, with a reduction in emphasis and activity in the other two markets.

It's also important to get to know what the priorities are and the critical success factors for this current year. This is not just for the individual product-market segments, but also at both the business unit and company level. Obviously, everyone in the business should understand this, but it's particularly important for the marketing team as they are creating medium-term investments to deliver against these priorities. You might even want to draft up an initial SWOT (strengths, weaknesses, opportunities and threats) of how you see the business and the environment facing you.

While you are taking this business snapshot you should also capture the picture of what you know about your territory. What resources have you got at your disposal, either directly or indirectly, particularly in terms of budgets and people? Capture your budget status as seen by the finance department. A simple example of this might be a target set at the start of the year, when specific rewards were put in place for sales-people to move certain products into certain markets: 'We must sell twice as many maintenance contracts at the point of purchase than we did last year, to make sure the maintenance team are producing the correct level of return.'

Week 3: Establish control

It's unlikely that you will be starting your new role with a completely clean sheet. More often than not you will be inheriting a 'patch', along with a set of existing or current activities. By week 3 you should aim to ensure that everything is under control. Just like taking over the controls of an aircraft, you quickly need to get a feel for what's going on, establish stability and get some visibility of the dashboard.

First, identify all the activities that are being worked on, along with all the outstanding commitments, whether to suppliers or internal and external customers. Review the status to ensure each is on track for delivery on time and within budget. It is critical that you demonstrate control of your budgets from the earliest stage. If you can't manage what you have, how will you expect the business to give you more to implement your plan moving forward? Also check, with your outsiders' perspective, that the activities are consistent and aligned both with each other and with the desired market positioning. Mark anomalies for further review and possibly put these on hold until that review.

Whether you have a clean sheet or not, you will need a management process to keep everything under control. See if what's in place is fit for purpose. The choice of email and spreadsheet or a more complete management tool is probably down to the size of the team and the number of activities. Don't decide on this management infrastructure issue at this point; just make sure everything on the horizon is under control and being delivered to plan.

QUICK TIP *GET A SIMPLE PRIORITISATION PROCESS*
Establish your own process for quickly getting everything
under control in a priority order. Memory joggers like the ABC
of first aid (airways, breathing and circulation) or the ANC of
flying (aviate, navigate and communicate) help to provide
clarity on important and urgent activities. I like ADA –
assemble (the facts and data), distil (the critical and relevant
points) and act. Or you might want to devise your own.

The priority this week is not only to make sure you are delivering against existing commitments, but also to establish a clearer picture of where you are currently heading. This is particularly important if you decide that a change of direction is required over the coming weeks. You will then be in a better position to assess the impact of any change and to integrate that into your plan.

Of course you might be in the lucky situation of having a brand new role – a green field opportunity with no legacy. If that's the case, then you could just accelerate your plan and define your approach to control later when you have an activity pipeline.

Week 4: Know and understand internal stakeholders

Some people might have stakeholder engagement further up the list, suggesting that you meet with them in the first couple of weeks, but I think that may be too early. That's not to say that these people are unimportant, but it goes back to the inside-out and outside-in thinking we discussed in Chapter 3. By spending the first three weeks meeting customers, understanding the business strategy and drivers, and getting your marketing territory under control, you are better equipped to enter into a valuable dialogue with stakeholders. While you are primarily seeking their perspective, you are now better informed about the external and internal realities, meaning you can engage more effectively.

You will no doubt have met many of your stakeholders already, but meetings in week 4 are an opportunity to sit down, hopefully face to face, for a quality discussion. Go into these meetings with your eyes open. Stop and think about each one. What role does each stakeholder play and how could they impact your success? What do you know about them already, what could go wrong and how can you mitigate any risks?

You might want to map out the stakeholders on an influencer map, as shown below, before and after the meetings, to help you monitor how relationships are panning out. Identify those stakeholders who have the greatest power or influence over your work. Think about who will be supportive and who will be less so. Consider how you can win round those who will oppose your ideas, as well as ways of using the support of your advocates. If you are managing a team, then remember that they are not only key to your success, but will also be interfacing with these stakeholders, potentially with their own agenda.

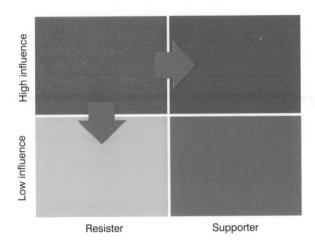

Your stakeholders might include your boss, your peers and team members, and influencers from functional areas such as sales, finance, product development and senior management. You may also consider stakeholders internal to your supply chain but external to the business, such as channel members, partners or suppliers. Use the meetings with these key people to understand their agendas, their concerns and their thoughts for the future. Try not to be drawn on stating your ideas at this stage, but equally don't be shy of entering into discussions on different perspectives and alternative approaches.

There is another objective from these meetings. You should be starting to assess these stakeholders, particularly your boss and your team, in terms of their capabilities, how they work and their ability to contribute to you and your plans. You could start to put together a draft SWOT of this extended team (see example overleaf). While the earlier SWOT focused on the bigger macro perspective, keep this analysis at the micro level – just on the people factors impacting you and your role.

Strengths	Weaknesses
The sales director believes that marketing can help her sell more There is a new and higher budget for marketing The marketing department has worked with the finance director before and has established a good relationship and common understanding of how marketing adds value to the business	Sales teams have often done their own thing in the past, running business development activities such as seminars and roadshows independently of marketing A new logo has been tried with poor results, so there is some confusion internally and externally Customer service teams have never worked with anyone from marketing to help to strengthen the customer relationship
Opportunities	**Threats**
A well researched marketing initiative will make selling easier Quick wins could enhance customer service and feed back into strong customer relationships The product range is fresh and relatively easy to enhance	A principle market is more or less saturated and any sales will be made on price Economic conditions are tight so customer spending could suffer and impact results A recent merger means that two competitors will together mount a major marketing campaign

At the end of the week develop a brief communication plan, based around the influencer map, that actively seeks the ongoing support for you and the team from all the highly influential stakeholders.

Week 5: Turn weaknesses or threats into some quick wins

By week 5 you should have gathered a picture of what is working and where the weak or broken links are in the marketing chain. At this stage you will want to take some action to repair weak or broken links. This does not mean a major programme that might pre-empt your medium-term plan, but some tactical action that will deliver quick wins.

Look at the entire sales funnel from the whole market, through suspects and prospects to customers both new and returning. You might see that marketing is generating lots of leads in the form of enquiries from sources such as the web or events, but that sales teams are not converting them effectively. Are you winning new customers but failing to keep existing ones? Or perhaps marketing and the business is failing to capture pertinent information about customers and their behaviour when presented with the opportunity. Quickly review performance through the awareness, interest, decision, action (AIDA) cycle and assess whether there is a 'weakest link' or bottleneck in the process. Alternatively, it might be something simple about how the team is working – an inefficient legacy process or perhaps time and effort wasted through duplication or non-productive activity.

Accept that you will not fix everything at once, but instead prioritise those areas you have spotted. By this point you will also have an understanding of the key business imperatives, some of which will no doubt incorporate revenue growth, profit improvement or market-share position management. The top priority weaknesses will be those that directly impact the performance against these key business drivers. Of these, pick one or two that will make a quick impact with minimum risk and disruption.

Effective quick wins might range from your insight as a new team member in identifying weaknesses, through to a workshop of key stakeholders to solve a problem. For example, perhaps you need a tactical promotional or incentive activity to unblock a customer bottleneck, if customers are delaying buying the existing product because they are aware that another is in the pipeline.

Suppose you have pinpointed a weakness in the attitude of the salespeople – what might you do? Identify a sales team, geographic or industry-specialised, sit down with them and agree where marketing can enhance what they are doing and areas where they might have to change their approach. Work on getting 20 per cent of the team to be more positive towards the marketing function and they will be your references as you try to eliminate that weakness.

 ### CASE STORY *MID-MARKET TEXTILE AND NAPERY BUSINESS, ADRIAN'S STORY*

Narrator Adrian is responsible for all marketing activity for this service-driven linen business.

Context As the new marketing person for a business selling linen to hotels, Adrian quickly implemented the development of a new website and a number of promotional activities. These proved to be extremely successful, with a flood of orders in the first month after launch.

Issue Adrian had not involved the purchasing and distribution department in his marketing plans and was unaware that sales had recently taken a major order to equip six new hotels. This meant that for people who had ordered on the internet the first contact they received from the company was a holding note saying that they could not deliver in the short term.

Solution Next time Adrian developed and launched a marketing promotional programme he included members of the sales and distribution departments in the planning, to make sure that the effort from the three departments was coordinated.

Learning Don't try to do marketing in isolation from the rest of the business. You run the risk of alienating internal groups, as well as setting incorrect expectations with customers.

Week 6: Set out your vision

You have now spent five weeks settling in, understanding the business and the people around you, and have started to make a difference to what and how marketing delivers for its customers. You should now have enough information and insight to put together a long-term vision for success – both yours and that of the business.

Take stock of where you are and reflect on what you have learnt. Then think about where you want to be and what you want to have achieved before you move on to your next role, whether that is in six months or several years. The clearer that you make this vision of what success looks like, the more likely it is that you will achieve it. Perhaps you could think about it in terms of the legacy that you would like to leave after you have moved on.

This vision will ultimately translate into your full plan, but in the meantime it will help you to set out what you intend to achieve and, perhaps just as importantly, what you're not going to do. Clarifying boundaries will help to focus you and your team, while ensuring that your limited resources and budget are not spread too thinly. Articulate what you see as the major opportunities and gaps, and how and when you intend to address each of them. This is not a detailed plan but a roadmap of where you want to get. Use it as a centrepiece for subsequent discussions with team members, your boss and other stakeholders.

You should also be thinking about how you intend to build your own capabilities, as well as those of your team, in order to make the vision a reality. Again, identify gaps and create personal development plans (PDPs) for everyone involved, so that you can harness strengths while eradicating weaknesses.

Make sure you have considered how compatible your vision and your way of life are. Ensure that you have factored in some level of balance between your work commitments and the demands of your preferred lifestyle. There is no point in doing a great job if you burn out in the next ten months!

Week 7: Develop your credibility and reputation

The first step in building the success you seek is to quickly establish a strong reputation. If your role is fundamentally different from your previous one, you might need to take a new approach and do things differently. If it's your first management role, then consider whether your team reports directly to you or whether there is more of a matrix structure with distributed specialists. The virtual teams of the matrix organisation are often more challenging to lead, so you may need to be sensitive and adapt your approach with the individual members in order to get the best from them. Remember that your personal reputation will now be dependent on the ability of the team to deliver results. This is particularly important in your first management role when, to a large extent, you switch from delivering results through your own efforts to achieving them through the expertise of others.

While you may manage your team directly with conventional reporting lines, many of the other resources you will require to be successful in your new marketing leadership role will be controlled by others outside the marketing arena, including sales, customer support and even finance. This means that you will need to use all the skills of influence in your armoury. A good reputation is a key asset that you need to develop to support this.

In addition to building your reputation with your team, you will want to think of the wider audience. Consider the various activities that you participate in on a regular basis and the impression you want to create at each. Think about internal events, such as management meetings or working with sales and other functional teams, and decide not just what you want from each one but also what you are able to contribute. You might want or need to act as a leader, an expert, a facilitator or a decision maker. Whichever you opt for, don't fall into the popular trap of talking too much for the sake of it!

As you build your reputation, so you should build your network. This will become more important as you become more senior. Initially you will have a lot of internal contacts, but you also need to look outside the company to recruit customers and partners as part of the network, as well as members from professional bodies. Investing time in building your network should prove fruitful from both personal and business perspectives. Again, look at how you can contribute to your network, as well as at how you can learn and benefit from it.

Week 8: Solicit input, ideas and feedback

The next week is critical, requiring a fine balance between authoritative and consensual leadership. You have set out your vision but you now need to start to turn that into an actionable plan. You need to generate ideas and options for the plan and at the same time take people with you, so the best approach is to seek input and feedback from those people. Ultimately, it is you who will decide on the plan, but the extended team will be invaluable in providing the creative ideas and input that are the raw elements in the mix.

You might want to seek one-to-one input from certain people, while some groups naturally lend themselves to a workshop environment where you can brainstorm and filter ideas. Either way, welcome input but keep your powder dry and reserve judgement on final decisions until you have finished all the idea gathering. At this stage you want ideas and options; decisions come next week.

QUICK TIP SOAK UP IDEAS

At this stage, just solicit ideas and input. Don't get into debates about pros and cons, ifs and buts, just get the ideas and feedback flowing. Think of this stage like a brainstorm where all inputs are valid until they are discussed at a later point.

By seeking active input you are also engaging with your various stakeholders, bringing them into the process and starting to get commitment and buy-in. This is important as it gives stakeholders a feeling of owner-ship for the plan, which helps during the eventual rollout. The trick, of course, is in managing the rejection of the ideas that don't make the plan, and the potential demotivation that could follow. As you start to put the plan together, try to communicate with contributors while focusing on the end goals for the business, so that everyone can see why some ideas are included and some are not. That way it is less about good and bad ideas, and more about overall fit and timing with the wider plan.

You should also be seeking feedback at this stage, not only on the vision and various ideas to implement it but also on your performance so far. Ask your boss for a formal review and find out what other stakeholders think about progress. You can also take a step back and give yourself a critical review. What has gone well in these first few weeks, what have you delivered against, and where have you failed to meet your expectations?

Week 9: Develop a medium-term plan

You now understand where the business is and what resources and capabilities you have at your disposal, and you have a vision of where you want to get to as well as a pool of creative ideas. It's now time to develop your medium-term plan. The actual time frame for the plan depends on your environment. In a fast-paced market, such as mobile phones, you might want to plan for a 9–18-month horizon. For industrial markets, such as heavy construction equipment or machine tools, you might feel that three or four years is a sensible medium-term time frame.

You might wish to start by revisiting and potentially updating your earlier vision. Perhaps you feel you could be more aggressive, or that you want to reduce the scope to focus your efforts on fewer, more critical elements. Work back from your end goals and identify what needs to be done and achieved on a month-by-month basis. Plan the activities for the first three to six months in detail. As the plan moves forward, you can then revisit and update the rolling horizon on a regular, probably monthly, basis.

Try to break the end goals down so that you can be as specific as pos-sible about shorter-term objectives and key performance indicators for the rollout of the plan. You and your stakeholders will want to know how to monitor progress and whether the plan is on track. For example, if you aim to increase market share from 14 per cent to 20 per cent over the two years, where would you expect to be after six months? How regularly is that information available from analysts following the market? Make sure that you include a range of leading indicators that capture market and financial markers as well as return on marketing investment (ROMI). Obvious, simple measures, such as marketing spend versus budget, will be part of your tracking, but make sure also to include more complex, difficult to access indicators, whether internal or external. These might include measures for channel or product mix, indicators for revenue pipeline and conversion, or new business versus repeat customers.

The plan should also identify potential barriers and risks that could derail your vision. It's unlikely that you will be able to capture everything, but try to think what could go wrong, what might trigger this and what you can do to stop it. Build the early indicators and the remedial actions for these risks into the plan.

Completing the plan is the start. Now you need to go and deliver against it.

Week 10: Energise yourself and your team for the road ahead

You have covered a lot of ground during the past nine weeks in the run-up to completing your medium-term plan. You have learnt a lot, started to build your reputation with influential stakeholders and set out a detailed campaign for the future. You now need to energise and get commitment from your extended team for the journey ahead.

Before you start implementing the activities, communicate the full plan to all the various interested parties. Seek their buy-in to the plan and their support in delivering their part of it. Not everyone will agree with all aspects, but aim to put across a balanced view so that they can see the bigger picture of what you are trying to achieve.

Next, you should aim to take time out for yourself and the team in order to prepare for the challenges and tasks ahead. As an obvious approach you might want to arrange a social evening where you can all let your hair down and get to know each other better. This might be done following a day or afternoon session going over the plan, getting everyone comfortable with what needs to be done when and by whom. If you go as far as a full-day workshop, you might want to close the loop from your first week and invite customers or business partners along to share their perspective with the whole team and even to provide reaction to your plans.

QUICK TIP *BRING THE TEAM ALONG*
As well as energising yourself, make sure you invigorate the team. Whether you have a team event off-site with some work and play, or a team dinner, share the energy, enthusiasm and ideas. Similarly, if you go to a conference or event then take a few team members as well. You will get much more value by discussing the ideas raised there as a team and you will also energise them by helping them to learn and develop.

A great way to get energised is to attend an appropriate event that stimulates your professional interest. You might have identified such an opportunity earlier, when assessing development needs. Make sure you and the team are now booked on to courses, seminars or workshops. I remember returning to the workplace from MBA seminars and courses with energy, ideas and enthusiasm. Other programmes that don't lead to formal qualifications can have the same effect. From simple things like assertiveness training, negotiation skills or finance basics for non-financial managers, through to more in-depth marketing training, people get energised from learning new things that they can apply to work and life. If you are new to a larger organisation, you might have more formal induction and training programmes set up for you. These often happen around this time and should provide you with another perspective on the organisation and its products.

With this energy, you should now be ready to take the next steps on your marketing Fast Track.

Checklist: what do I need to know?

During the first ten weeks in your new role, start gathering information that will help you to deliver results, build your team and develop your career. Use the following checklist to see whether you have the necessary information – using a simple Red-Amber-Green status, where Red reflects major gaps in current knowledge and suggests immediate action is required, Amber suggests some knowledge is missing and may need to be addressed at some stage in the future, and Green indicates you are happy with the current state.

TOPIC	INFORMATION	RAG
Business context	The major trends in the industry that will impact what you do, how you do it and your marketing priorities	
Business strategy	The overall strategy for the business in terms of its products and markets and the basis on which it differentiates itself in the market	
Team objectives	The key performance indicators (KPIs) that will be used to assess whether you and your team have been a success	
Stakeholders	Those individuals or groups that you will work with and that will influence the success or failure of your marketing activities	
The team	Individual members of your marketing team – their names, their backgrounds and their relative strengths and weaknesses	
Roles	The roles and responsibilities within marketing that are needed to deliver results – internal to the team or external contributors	
Customers	Your top five internal or external customers and their specific needs and wants	
Suppliers	Your key marketing agencies – who they are and how they contribute to the success of your team	
Your boss	Your operational manager – who they are, their preferred style and what it is that really makes them tick	
The director	The person leading marketing activities within the business, and possibly the person whose job you aspire to	
Key opinion leaders	People across the organisation whose expert knowledge and opinion is respected by others – who they are and what they each have to offer	
Current commitments	The current operational marketing activities – what they are and what it will take to make them succeed	
Future workload	Future expectations in terms of what needs to be delivered when and by whom	
Budget	The amount of funding available for marketing activities – where this will come from and what the sign-off process is	
Resources	The people, facilities, equipment, materials and information available to you for your activities	
Scope	The boundaries that have been set for you and your team – the things you are not allowed to do	

TOPIC	INFORMATION	RAG
Key events	The major events that are happening within the business that will influence what you need to do and when	☐
Potential problems	The risks you face going forward – the things that could go wrong based on the assumptions you have made	☐
SWOT	The relative strengths, weaknesses, opportunities and threats for your marketing team	☐
Review process	The formal review process for your internal team reviews, at which KPIs will be reviewed with your boss	☐

STOP – THINK – ACT

After reading this chapter you will be aware of how critical the first ten weeks in a new role can be to success, and that there are a number of actions that you should take to increase your chances of success. Take time now to reflect on each of these ideas and put together a plan for your first ten weeks.

What should I do?	What do I need to achieve?
Who do I need to involve?	Who needs to be involved and why?
What resources will I require?	What information, facilities, materials, equipment or budget will be required?
What is the timing?	When will tasks be achieved?
	Week 1
	Week 2
	Week 3
	Week 4
	Week 5
	Week 6
	Week 7
	Week 8
	Week 9
	Week 10

Visit www.Fast-Track-Me.com to use the Fast Track online planning tool.

EXPERT VOICE

Key trends in advertising
Professor Douglas West

Over the past ten years there has been a significant shift from 'push' to 'pull' marketing strategies that has had a major impact on advertising. Push is when advertisers place information in order to influence, whereas pull is when the audience pulls information towards itself. Generally the shift from push to pull has been viewed as a shift in power to the consumer away from advertisers and so is 'bad news' for marketers.

Nevertheless, there are a number of benefits. For example, inventory may be reduced, as with Dell only making a laptop when it is ordered and paid for. Pull interactions also enable producers to identify individuals and thereby target and tailor goods and services to the micro rather than macro level.

Overall, the result has been a general shift away from mass communications, leading to what might be loosely termed 'demassification' and a tendency towards integration of media campaigns.[1] Many leading advertisers have shifted their budgets away from advertising towards sharper-focused media, such as in-store video networks, the web and specialist magazines, and attempts to create 'buzz'.[2] In order to survive, the traditional mass media have fragmented at a rapid rate, particularly as the part played by mass campaigns has changed to a support role – with press advertisements exhorting the use of a website where the real 'selling' will take place.

Despite the rise of digital media and the shift from push to pull, there is some evidence that homes with digital video recorders watch slightly more commercials than those without. This is because DVR households tend to watch more television, and partly because time-shifting simply means they still watch the commercials, albeit later. A study in 2007,[3] using in-home cameras in eight households, found the vast majority of viewers with DVRs still watched programmes in real time, and even when they did fast-forward recordings they still recognised the commercials.

[1] McGrath, John M. (2005), 'IMC at a crossroads: a theoretical review and a conceptual framework for testing', *Marketing Management Journal*, 15(2), 55–66.

[2] Thomas Jr., Greg Metz (2004), 'Building the buzz in the hive mind', *Journal of Consumer Behaviour*, 4(1) 64–72.

[3] Pearson, S. and Barwise, P. (2007), 'DVRs and advertising exposure: a video ethnographic study', *International Journal of Internet Marketing and Advertising*, 4(1), 93–113.

Another key trend has been a general movement to measure results, particularly in terms of return on investment (ROI). To some extent measurement has not helped the mass media, as their value is difficult to measure because it is generally realised in the long run and related to brand equity, which is hard to establish. For example, major network TV advertising for O2 has greatly enhanced the brand over several years but is difficult to measure in the immediate duration or 'halo' of the campaign. To be fair, even more measurable media, such as the web, have their problems. In particular, online 'pay per click' frauds in the USA have cost advertisers millions, as even the most vigilant search engine will have trouble unearthing fraud.

Rating points are the common currency to measure the exposure obtained on TV, but this is not the same as impact. A rating point measures the percentage of the potential audience exposed at a given time or over the life of a campaign. Points can relate to the audience as a whole or to a particular demographic segment. For example, in the UK on a combined daily basis ITV1, C4 and Five reach about 55 per cent of men, 60 per cent of women and nearly 35 per cent of children. However, a show with a low overall rating may be better than a show with a much larger one because it reaches a particular segment that advertisers might be aiming for. For instance, in the USA the Fox Network has been extremely successful at delivering highly sought-after viewers, albeit in relatively small numbers.

New media measurement systems are underway – for example, in 2007 Unilever and Proctor & Gamble joined forces in the USA with 'Project Apollo' in an attempt to develop close to single-source data. The project, conducted by AC Nielsen and Arbitron, involved 14,000 people who carried mobile phone-sized 'people meters', which recorded their exposure to all electronic media, TV, radio, iPods, cinema and the web, while exposure to print and direct marketing was covered by surveys. All were linked to purchasing data.

LEADING THE TEAM

Leadership skills are as important to reaching your goals as gaining expert knowledge and being familiar with appropriate tools and techniques. Focus on your personal attributes as a marketing leader, reflecting on what it takes to lead and develop a team to achieve both short- and long-term success.

Changing myself

How should I think?

The obvious reply to this is to think like a leader, but there is a bit more to it than that. Take a close look at yourself. Reflect on your self-perception and on your strengths and weaknesses. What do you recognise? How does that perception and how do those characteristics match up with the role you have taken on? At question here are not so much your actual traits but your recognition of them. At a conference I recently attended, one speaker had identified and classified entrepreneurs as one of four types. In their desire to want to fit the 'classic' entrepreneur profile, many of the audience missed the point and asked questions about how they should develop these classic traits, rather than accept the profile they had. It's a bit like finding out your blood group and then wanting it to be something different. We will come later to attitude and behaviours, but as for personality types – recognise what you have and work with it.

New roles should be an interesting challenge, but the jump into your first management role is probably the most significant for you in terms of the level of change required. How often do we hear people reflecting on how the top performing individuals – whether in sales, engineering, marketing or any other area – do not necessarily make the best managers? As a new marketing leader, you now need to lead, motivate and support others to come up with sound analyses, strategies and plans, as well as with well-executed, on-time, in-budget programmes, rather than just doing it yourself. This may sound attractive, but many find delegation harder than they thought. The first issue that people experience is the new distance between themselves and former peers, which shouldn't necessarily be a major stumbling block but is certainly a point of difference.

Thinking as a marketing leader is probably going to require you to adapt. You need to be more aware of the bigger picture than you were before, whether that is across the organisation or from the perspective of the market as a whole. This means being more proactive in terms of anticipating change. One of the key attributes of the Fast Track manager is that they spend more time looking up and around them at what is happening in other functions or businesses. You need to be more commercial, with an eye on the bottom line, cost control and efficient operations. You also need to work out what traits you have that will make people want to follow you.

Being good at managing yourself builds confidence both for yourself and for those around you. So if you can exhibit attributes such as good time management, focus, planning and personal development, it will set the tone for the team culture, as the people around you recognise these strengths.

A useful idea is to do a self-assessment against the four categories of knowledge, competencies, attitudes and behaviours. Do you have the necessary **knowledge** about changes in the industry, your top customers and your major competitors? Do you have the **competencies** to think creatively, conduct analyses to understand why things happen (or could happen) and put into place plans that will deliver benefits on time and within budget? Do you have the right **attitude** in terms of being positive, seeking synergies between people's ideas and constantly looking for breakthroughs? Do you recognise and reward those involved with creating such breakthoughs, even with something as simple as a thank you? And do you actively support others through the marketing process, and **behave** as someone that people want to turn to for help?

Use a structured approach to identify specific areas in each of these four categories that you feel you need to work on. Take time to discuss your thoughts with your boss or your coach. You could summarise your thoughts in the form of a SWOT analysis. Depending on the change required, you could incorporate this thinking into your development plan, or alternatively just do it. It might just be a question of practising a new behaviour, or starting to read that collection of books to improve your knowledge.

What leadership style is appropriate?

QUICK TIP STYLE
You will naturally have your own approach to leading people. Try to recognise your leadership style as well as that of the organisation you're in. Hopefully there is a match, but remember that you may need to flex your style to get the best out of people or simply to get the job done. Different teams and different activities often require different approaches to maximise performance, so consider whether a change would suit your circumstances.

Whether, like most readers, these are your first exploratory steps into management, or you are an experienced manager looking to reinvigorate your career in marketing, it's worth taking time to reflect on what leadership style is most appropriate for you and your environment. One way of thinking about this is to consider the extent to which you involve others in key events and decisions. One extreme is to be dictatorial and adopt a 'command' style, where you make the decisions in isolation without involving or consulting others. For example, you may decide what the key priorities are and simply tell people to get on with implementing them. At the other extreme you involve the group in deciding areas to focus on through a consensus-driven approach. There are, of course, stages between the two. You may choose to ask questions of key team members, whether peers or potentially people working for you, in order to confirm facts such as the threat from the competition, or you may consult them individually or as a group and ask their opinion – but then still make the decisions yourself. This model of leadership is effectively a continuum from command to consensus (see figure), and there are examples where each has been used very effectively.

There are examples of very successful organisations that operate at each point on this continuum, but it is worth remembering that marketing is a discipline of influence, which by definition implies that where possible you might want to take people with you on a journey rather than dictate. And it's not just your marketing team to which this applies. You also need to demonstrate leadership to other internal groups, such as sales teams or the finance department.

Different leadership approaches suit different circumstances, depending on the balance of time or speed to decision, the commitment and buy-in of the various stakeholders and the quality of the decision. Fast Track marketing leaders assess each situation quickly and are then flexible enough to adapt their style based on these criteria.

By moving towards the consensus end of the spectrum and increasing the number of people involved with decision making, it naturally takes longer to reach a conclusion. Sometimes action needs to be taken quickly, so a more autocratic style is needed. That must be balanced with the fact that the more involved people feel, the more likely they are to commit to decisions and actively support the implementation of ideas (see figure below). The quality of the decision making is crucial. There is no point in making decisions in isolation if you lack the facts or experience. You will simply be inviting the introduction of errors, risking the failure of the initiative and exposing your reputation. At the same time, if you are to allow the team carte blanche to make key decisions and to set priorities, you need to make sure that whatever they come up with will be acceptable to the business.

Time invested and speed   Commitment to decision

Quality

Teams get used to a manager's style and often adapt their behaviour to conform, or perhaps move out if they don't like it. Once they have acclimatised to your style, it is likely to cause confusion and discomfort if you change it significantly without extenuating circumstances. Of course, you will change your style according to the situation and they will appreciate that and understand why you are doing it. You can't use a collaborative style during the heat of a major event when swift action is needed to divert a crisis – for example, a key customer cancelling at short notice their commitment to address the salespeople at a conference. But it is appropriate to spend time with the team after the event to review and discuss how to avoid such a crisis next time.

Fast Track marketing managers will be skilled and comfortable operating at all points on the continuum as the situation demands. You will need to be able to:

→ **Command.** Analyse the situation, solve problems, make decisions and proactively think ahead and manage risks on your own.

→ **Question.** Ask open and closed questions and, crucially, listen to the answers without interrupting, to the point where you have sufficient facts to make the decision.

→ **Consult.** Be able and willing to listen hard to what others are telling you, and be sensitive enough to pick up on the subtler signals such as feelings and opinions.

→ **Collaborate.** Manage meetings effectively with clear objectives, agenda and logistics. Be willing to challenge the group and manage conflict where there are differences of opinion.

→ **Consensus.** Set group boundaries, build consensus in a team and gain commitment to outputs. The key point is that not everyone needs to agree with the decision of the group, but they do need to commit to it.

Motivating the individual

How do I get the most out of each member of my marketing team?

Whether it's the people in your team reporting directly to you or simply contributors and stakeholders elsewhere in the business, you will need to keep them motivated in order to maximise their contribution. Motivation can be derived from many sources, including the challenge of the task, the dynamics of the team or a belief in the vision. Human psychologists suggest that motivation and behaviours are driven by the antecedents that set the scene beforehand and the consequences that people expect afterwards from exhibiting desired behaviours (see figure).

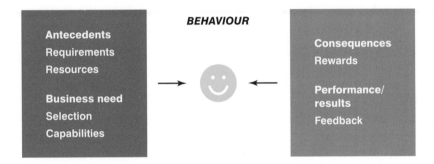

→ **Antecedents**. Are all the ingredients in place to facilitate the behaviours and ultimately the performance you are looking for? Is there a clear and well-articulated business need driving the marketing aspect of the task or activity to hand? It is a poor antecedent if people do not see a customer need or their own organisation's interests behind a marketing decision or event. In these cases, they will not be very motivated to follow your guidelines. The militaristic chain of command approach – expecting someone to do something just because you have told them to – works less well in commercial life: it only really works in military life because the consequences of non-compliance are undesirable. People will be much more motivated and perform better if they understand the reasons and the need for the activity. This also applies to the clarity of the requirements. Does everyone understand the scope and specification of the activity? Of course the team also needs appropriate resources to be able to deliver the results required. These might include sufficient time, budget, information, facilities and other people. There is nothing less motivating after planning or even starting a marketing campaign than to be told that the budget has been cut by 15 per cent this quarter but that you still need to deliver the same results. No wonder people tend to inflate budgets with contingency! Finally, you need to match the right activities with the people who have the appropriate capabilities. Individual team members have different strengths and weaknesses and will expect you to recognise those. Either select people with strengths in the required area or acknowledge that you see this as a development opportunity. Don't just throw people into the deep end and expect them to swim without some support.

→ **Consequences**. Look closely at the tasks and activities and assess the natural consequences for each person. What happens if they do a great job and meet or exceed the performance requirements? What tangible or visible benefits do they receive? Avoid situations where there are positive consequences for doing a bad job. Also recognise that an approach based on fear is unlikely to produce sustainable results, but be prepared to use consequences to eliminate poor behaviours. For example, nominate late arrivals for meetings to carry out tasks such as note-taking. In general, though, focus on how you drive positive behaviour with positive outcomes. Consequences will focus on a combination of rewards and feedback. Rewards cover a wide range of financial or non-financial options, from increased visibility with senior management for a job well done, through a range of small incentives right up to stock options or promotions. Feedback can be equally powerful, even at the level of taking the time to offer a simple 'Thank you for a great job'. Also consider how you would like to encourage certain behaviours, such as effective teamwork, that do not necessarily show up directly in the results. You could reward the team with a dinner or evening out to celebrate success.

QUICK TIP CLEAR MESSAGES

Whether the environment is encouraging or dictatorial, team or individually oriented, results or process driven, make sure that everyone knows what is expected of them and the consequences of their behaviour and performance.

Think about the team activities and campaigns during the next quarter and the individuals delivering against those. What do you need to put in place in terms of antecedents, and what do you need to do to ensure that the consequences of performing are positive ones?

Create the right environment

Why is this important?

Antecedents and consequences are the starting point in setting the right environment for sustainable performance from your team or the marketing function. It's critically important to develop a culture of success, both inside the team and also among key stakeholders outside the team so that everyone sees the contribution.

The group or team culture cuts across everything, from the physical environment to the attitudes and behaviours of all the team members. As the leader you have the opportunity to create and shape the culture of your team, even if you have limited capacity to do the same across the wider organisation. Having said that, it is an important role of marketing to break down departmental barriers and make sure that staff right across the organisation can see the relevance and benefits of marketing – achieve this and their cooperation will follow naturally.

CASE STORY *SUN MICROSYSTEMS, LES'S STORY*

Narrator Les was a business development manager, coordinating sales and marketing activity across a number of markets.

Context At the turn of the millennium Sun was riding the crest of a wave, selling computer systems to businesses to run their critical processes, store their precious data and harness the power of the internet. Growth was strong and many in the business portrayed a sense of invincibility. However, the crash following the end of the dotcom boom highlighted the stark reality.

Issue A number of people in senior and middle management positions reacted to the downturn with classic, knee-jerk thinking, resorting to micro-management and an inconsistent, short-term mindset. The business was in danger of lurching from one crisis to the next as a result of 'flavour of the week' management by some senior 'leaders'.

Solution Fortunately the management chain in Les's area included some of the best people in the industry. Diane and Steve, his direct bosses, were great leaders who were motivated and motivating. They set clear boundaries and expectations, while providing a large amount of autonomy for Les to get on with the job on a day-to-day basis.

Learning Getting the balance right in leading people is always difficult. Teams will generally respond well to consistency, mutual respect, honesty and openness, but these important factors become even more critical when times get tough. At that point, despite the short-term attractions of autocracy and micro-management for weak managers, people will perform better under an open but fair and firm management style.

What culture is best?

There is no single right answer to this. It will vary depending on your pre-ferred style and the business context or situation at a point in time. However, research has shown that there are some basic components that encourage an environment that will be more conducive to sustained performance and qualities such as innovation, entrepreneurial ideas, creativity and commercial orientation.

→ **Creative challenge**. Aim to create an environment of positive challenge and confrontation. It is easy to knock an idea, so make sure that people have an alternative or are prepared to search for one. The idea is not to knock ideas but to challenge constructively. Encourage people to question and to justify. When done positively this not only builds teamwork and puts energy into proceedings, but also gets everyone engaged. You want engaged people working on your team, as these are the people who are looking to transform the business and your position in the market. Two other types that you are less keen to have as part of the team could be seen as 'tourists' and 'terrorists'. The former tend to watch as proceedings pass by but don't really engage, while terrorists are the people who believe they have more important things to do and so bring a very negative attitude to the party. Try instead to encourage as many as possible to be transformers.

→ **Blame-free**. Any organisation that wants to move forward has to accept that failures do happen. Failure is a common factor in many entrepreneurial success stories. Nowhere is this more apparent that with the ups and downs of a Formula One motor racing team – always pushing the envelope, celebrating success but learning from problems rather than finger-pointing when failures happen. Some might say that fortunately marketing is a less stressful environment. But the same principles apply. Everything we do in life brings with it a degree of uncertainty and risk, and the harder we push the more likely it is that something will go wrong. In a competitive environment, however, we have to push, and we have to accept that we can't always get it right, but if people are heavily criticised for getting it wrong then they will quickly stop pushing for fear of being ridiculed. Just as in life and childhood, learning from mistakes and avoiding blame is an extremely powerful approach for developing both individuals and the organisation.

→ **Not too proud**. Avoid the 'not invented here' syndrome and recognise that many of the best ideas will be developed outside your organisation or team. Accept it and harness it. The development of the internet, the availability of information and the networks of people and businesses have introduced new possibilities for working. Historically, only those organisations that could invest a significant amount of funds into research and development (R&D) would create new products. Now a new way of working, referred to as search and development (S&D), makes a clear statement to all stakeholders that it's OK to reuse the ideas of others. Many very successful businesses, and not just from low-wage economies, are based on this copy or 'white-label'/non-branded model. As a marketing team you need to understand the impact of this on you. You might be on one or both sides of the divide between copier or copied, white-label or brand. Whichever, you need to recognise it, foster a culture where you don't expect to have a monopoly on bright ideas and be prepared to borrow appropriate ideas. Even if you are not replicating products, you should copy ideas and process-improvement opportunities.

→ **Ethical boundaries**. Make a choice about what you will and will not be prepared to consider in terms of marketing activity. This applies to which product categories you offer and markets you address. But it also applies to what and how you market those products to the customers you target. Obvious examples of ethical boundaries for businesses and marketing teams include involvement with the arms and tobacco industries, and the marketing of foods that do little to reduce the growing obesity problem. As well as making a statement about your beliefs – what is right and what is wrong – you will clarify the boundaries for others. In any industry there will be the possibility of cutting corners, flirting with legality and behaving in a more or less green manner. Think about the issues that affect you and your industry and make decisions on the limits you will set.

→ **Learning organisation**. Work hard to create a culture where people learn from each other and from the past. While it is important to keep moving forward and accept failure, it will demotivate people to see a new idea fail badly in the market-place, only to discover that someone else had already made the very same mistake several years earlier. This is a discipline that needs to be built into the culture of the team. A mobile phone manufacturer developed a new phone that combined advanced software with the latest thin-screen technology to create a display that was second to none. Unfortunately it quickly became clear that the mechanism for embedding the display in the phone was faulty, and almost 50 per cent of the phones had to be recalled. This cost the business approxi-mately $5 million in rejects and $5 million in terms of the adverse impact on the brand. But in the spirit of the blame-free culture, the senior management team stated that this was understandable for a leading technology company – there would be some failures. However, nine months later the upgrade to the phone was released, and while it had some highly innovative new features, it still had the same fault as the original phone. Although this is a product example, it relates closely to product marketing and marketing itself, and as such highlights the lessons that need to be captured and not repeated across the whole of the marketing arena.

What should the physical environment look like?

You should aim for an energised, creative environment that encourages teamwork while allowing space for thinking and reflection. Marketing is a multifaceted discipline that at different times requires creativity, analysis, strategic thinking, frantic action and reflection. So you want an environment where the team can undertake all these activities easily. From a buildings and facilities perspective, that might involve a combination of open-plan and individual offices. There are examples of work environments that include Nintendo Wii, lounge areas, table football tables or even areas suit-able for a quick nap. These might or might not be appropriate for your business, but do try to avoid austere, dull, poorly lit, energy-sapping envi-ronments if you expect your marketing team to perform.

Whatever the physical environment, as a team leader you need to be accessible for support, advice, comment or guidance. Enlightened management used to call this an 'open-door' policy, but today anyone not operating like this as a matter of course probably shouldn't be in management.

Of course, with the advances in technology, you should also be prepared for the possibility that the team is rarely together in one place but distributed at remote offices, home offices or even 'on the road'. IT and telecommunications technology means that this is not only feasible but also generally seamless. For management, remote working teams bring additional challenges – not from a performance perspective but from a bonding and relationship perspective. In these circumstances, how do you harness the power of teamworking and the associated synergies when you have a bunch of individuals working remotely? If necessary, bring the team together at appropriate opportunities and venues to celebrate success, share ideas, align and plan future activities and – just as importantly – to bond.

Building the team

What makes a great team?

So you have a great leadership style that is flexible enough to cope with different situations, and you have a number of highly motivated and skilled people to work with, but that does not necessarily make them a great team. So what factors are needed to create great teams – ones that are distinctly different from average ones or ones that are made up of a bunch of excellent individuals? In the sporting world, there has been media comment that the US team in Ryder Cup golf matches has too often failed to gel as a team despite being comprised of a large number of top-ranked players. How do you harness the synergies to bring that something extra, so that 2 + 2 equals 5 rather than 3 or 4? During my time in corporate life, working in a wide variety of teams, I can honestly say that synergy was only harnessed and developed on two occasions to produce truly great teams and environments. However, just because it's rare doesn't mean that you shouldn't be aiming to find that extra ingredient to make a great team.

QUICK TIP *TEAM ADJUSTMENT*
When a key member of the team moves on, you need to be like a Premiership football team that has sold its best player – regroup and show how the team will operate differently but just as successfully.

Read through the following checklist and reflect on what you need to do as leader of the team in order to ensure success.

→ **The team will have great clarity in its goals and have a real sense of purpose.** Fast Track teams will have a vision that they will want to be remembered for, both among themselves and as a legacy for the business. Whether it's through an entry into a new market, a product launch, a period of sustained growth or a breakthrough campaign, the team is probably seeking to transform the company's fortunes.

→ **The team will have a strong and enthusiastic leader.** This leader provides direction, is supportive of team members and is willing to shoulder responsibility when things do not go according to plan. They are often not the expert or specialist, but they understand how to bring people together and get them to perform effectively as a unit.

→ **Fast Track teams also accept that things change and can act flexibly in order to bring things back on track.** People come and go for a variety of reasons, and competitors try to move the goalposts, but the team will work together to re-appraise the situation quickly and calmly, exploring creative options for dealing with the situation and getting on with it.

→ **They will have shared values and a common set of operating principles.** While teams comprise people with a variety of skills and experiences, they need to be unified by common beliefs that can provide them with enormous energy and commitment.

→ Ideally, those shared values then extend into a general respect and liking for each other, where team members trust each other and genuinely have fun working together. This might happen naturally but can also be assisted by quality team-building activities, such as off-sites that create shared experiences.

→ **Open and honest communication through the team will help to ensure that any issues that arise will be dealt with quickly and sensitively before they become crises.** A blame-free environment without finger pointing is an integral part of this.

→ **While these teams will focus on their primary objectives, they will take time out to learn and develop new skills continually.** Whether that learning is from operational successes and failures, or from the developmental needs of the team and the individuals, everyone will always be looking to improve.

→ **Finally, the team will be balanced.** Perhaps in the short term you need to work with what you have, but a great team will have a balance in terms of the skills and capabilities, working styles and personality types. It's important to try to map these factors against the roles performed by the team to optimise the performance of the whole. Ideally, you will need creative ideas people as well as people willing to get their heads down in order to put the work in and deliver the results.

How should I develop the team?

As well as developing individual skills, you need to forge a cohesive team. Review the list of attributes of a great team above and make a note of any area where you feel there is a need for improvement.

Although we talk of the marketing team as a single, unified entity, recognise that you could actually have a disparate group of functional specialists who may have little in common apart from the fact they have the same boss. However, that doesn't mean that they can't and shouldn't still operate as a team with some common goals.

You might want to assess where you think the team is in terms of their stage of development. Teams go through various stages of development, and your role as the leader will be to recognise where they are and to take action to move them to a state where they are at their most productive. Consider the extended Tuckman[1] model:

[1] Concept developed by Bruce Wayne Tuckman in the short article 'Developmental sequence in small groups', 1965 (**www.infed.org/thinkers/tuckman.htm**).

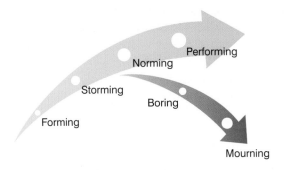

As a leader you need to be aware of these phases and be able to manage the team through them. Try to keep energy levels high after the early forming and storming stages. Quickly establish norming behaviours so that everyone knows what is expected of them, and monitor and feed back performance so that the performing stage is optimised and extended. Recognise if the group or individuals are moving into a boring phase, and either refresh, challenge and energise them or plan for managing an ultimate departure from the team.

STAGE	DESCRIPTION	LEADERSHIP ACTIONS
Forming	The group is brought together for the first time and needs to start understanding each other and what they each contribute. Perhaps the team is comprised of people from distinct functions such as PR, product marketing, marketing communications and events.	Although the functions might be different, try to balance the team in terms of personalities, styles, skills and experience. Allow people to get to know each other personally and set simple tasks to allow people to work together for the first time and get quick group wins.
Storming	Initially they will each be keen to contribute and have their say, perhaps establishing a pecking order as to who has the greatest sway over the outcomes. Manage this carefully, as teams can become very 'political' if individuals jockey for power and positions. This can result in a downward spiral in terms of effectiveness, so again strive for balance.	Make sure the team is set up to achieve early successes. Communicate team roles clearly so that everyone knows what their contribution is. There will always be the potential for conflict, so look for it and seek consensus on key decisions at an early stage.

STAGE	DESCRIPTION	LEADERSHIP ACTIONS
Norming	As things settle down, the team will need to adopt norms in terms of how it works together, including decision making, communication and meeting disciplines. Without common processes a lot of the energy and enthusiasm of the team can be dissipated.	Communicate your leadership style. Let them know under what circumstances you will seek the team's views and how you expect them to work.
Performing	The team should now have clear roles and be working effectively as a unit. This is where results are produced, and you need to keep the team in this positive and effective mode.	Monitor performance regularly and take swift action to resolve issues before they become crises. Spend one-on-one time with each member of the team to keep them motivated.
Boring	For teams that have been together for a long time, there is a danger that they stop challenging the way they work. This can happen to teams and individuals who get into a rut after being in a role for a long time. If left unchecked, this can result in the team or members getting bored, and performance can quickly degrade.	Find ways of constantly challenging the team as a whole and as individuals. Consider bringing in new members or rotating jobs and roles. Perhaps there will come a point where you need to fundamentally adjust the team's objectives in order to get them to stop and re-evaluate what they are doing.
Mourning	Finally, for high-performing teams, there is always a major sense of loss when a valued member or perhaps the business moves on, requiring changes. Following significant change or new members joining, the team in effect moves back into the 'forming' stage.	When people leave the team, for good or bad reasons, think carefully about the transition. Focus on some of the softer people issues within the team – not simply on updating the plan.

QUICK TIP USE CHANGE TO ENERGISE
Don't change things for the sake of it but encourage the team to create change internally and externally. Draw energy and revitalisation from change.

How do I overcome barriers to change?

Change is the one constant and will affect both the team and the business. So it is crucial that you learn to embrace change and have strategies in place to overcome any resistance to change. As the team leader, you should establish that change is a way of life, so it is counterproductive to resist it. A Fast Track manager that I worked with in the early stages of my marketing career had an appropriate reminder pinned to his board: 'Those that are successful have one thing in common: they create change rather than react to it!'

This thinking should fit well with someone who has chosen a career in marketing because this discipline is about creating changes in perceptions and markets. However, when change impacts the team it can be more difficult to embrace. Sometimes there is resistance simply because certain individuals do not like change. But once people recognise that change is inevitable and that it's pointless resisting, it becomes much easier to reduce the barriers that can appear.

As the marketing team leader you might need to implement all types of change: redundancies or budget cuts, team merging and integration, bringing in new working practices or systems. The denial, resistance, exploration and commitment (DREC) change model (see figure) can help you to understand the process that people need to go through and can give insights in terms of what you will need to consider when planning changes.

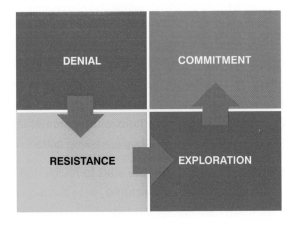

→ **Denial**. People refuse to accept that the change will happen. It might be a difficult change – for example, where in-house functions are now being outsourced to agency partners. There may be cries of 'It will never work because …' coming from different teams. Many organisations regularly fail to implement changes effectively, and the organisation might then revert back to its former state quite quickly. It is perhaps no wonder that people are often cynical about change and will wait to see whether anything actually happens. To be taken seriously you have to drive the change through. Accept that some people will be in denial, but find a way of helping them to come to terms with the fact that the change will happen.

→ **Resistance**. Even once people have accepted that the change will happen, many are still resistant. It is their way of telling you that they are still not convinced that this is the right way to go. Take time to explain the business case for the change, making it clear why the current situation will not endure. Also discuss why this approach has been chosen as the optimum or only solution. Identify those people in the business who have bought in to the idea and who are also widely respected – we call them the key opinion leaders. Use these people to spread the word and explain to others why this change is so vital for the future. Experience has shown that if 20 per cent of key opinion leaders are positive about the change, you will probably be able to drive it through; with less than that you may have problems to overcome.

→ **Exploration**. Once there is an acceptance that the change will happen and that it is a good thing, allow people to investigate ways in which it will impact them and their teams for the better, and ways in which they can help with implementation. Get them involved and make sure they are taking action.

→ **Commitment**. Finally, as people start to realise the benefits, take time to capture the early victories, write them up and communicate them across other teams. Just as you would communicate to the market about early successes with a new product, it is hugely beneficial to bring the internal audience along with you during change programmes. Sometimes those that showed the greatest level of resistance, once converted, become your best advocates.

The DREC cycle is a useful way of understanding the natural stages we all go through when faced with change. Some of us will move through the cycle much faster than others, so take time early on to help those who are struggling to move through.

STOP – THINK – ACT

This chapter has presented ideas for managing and developing your team. This will be key to your success, as you will not be able to achieve your objectives working alone. Marketing is often most effective where cross-functional teams, in which you will not necessarily have direct control, are pulled together to achieve a breakthrough. Whether in this matrix structure or a dedicated marketing group, team working and effective leadership are essential.

Reflect on how well you are leading the team and look for ways you could improve. Now think about how well the team is operating – is it balanced and operating as a cohesive unit? What groups affected by change are not in the 'committed' section of the DREC model? Where is the team along the 'forming to mourning' model?

What should we do?	What actions do we need to take to build the team?
Who do we need to involve?	Who needs to be involved and why?
What resources will we require?	What level of investment would be required?
What is the timing?	What deadlines do we need to meet?

Visit **www.Fast-Track-Me.com** to use the Fast Track online planning tool.

EXPERT VOICE

Measuring is good; measuring what matters might be even better

Professor John Roberts and Pamela Morrison

For the past few years the top industry–academic liaison body in marketing, the Marketing Science Institute, has had marketing metrics as its top priority. The logic is good. In an era of evidence-based management with a mantra 'If you can't measure it, you can't manage it', marketing is being forcibly asked to justify investments that have been made to understand, provide value to and capture economic rents from consumers.

It is hard to argue against such pressure and indeed considerable progress is being made to satisfy it. For those interested in measures of marketing success, books by Paul Farris and his colleagues and by John Davis provide excellent compendia of useful metrics.[2] As far as the frameworks that unite these measures and tie marketing inputs to financial outcomes, both Tim Ambler and Pat LaPointe have published guides giving practical advice.[3] Finally, templates to report progress towards marketing objectives that enable evaluation of past performance and improved planning and resource allocation for future performance can be found in a software/hardware combination by Roger Best.[4]

This is all laudable, but we would like to sound three notes of warning. The first is that of completeness. Many effects in marketing are observable and readily calibrated. Sales response to impulse advertising is one example of this. Other effects are more indirect and their impact is felt over a long period of time. Brand-building advertising might be regarded as an example of the latter. There is a substantial body of research that demonstrates the strong and significant carry-over effects of advertising. The best outcome is that the manager has a good handle on both types of effect and then factors both (perhaps discounted by different rates because of different business risk) into the optimal marketing expenditure decision. A particularly dangerous outcome, often worse than no quantitative analysis at all, is that inputs are allocated to maximise only directly observable effects. That must

---

[2] Farris, P., Bendle, N., Pfeifer, P. and Reibstein, D. (2007), *Marketing Metrics: 50+ Metrics Every Executive Should Master*, Philadelphia: Wharton School Publishing; Davis, J. (2007), *Measuring Marketing: 103 Key Metrics Every Marketer Needs*, Singapore: John Wiley.

[3] Ambler, T. (2003), *Marketing and the Bottom Line*, Harlow: Pearson Education; LaPointe, P. (2007), *Marketing by the Dashboard Light*, New York: Association of National Advertisers.

[4] Best, Roger (2005), *Market Based Management: Strategies for Growing Customer Value and Profitability*, 4th edn, Upper Saddle river NJ: Pearson Education.

lead to under-investment (by an average amount related to the value of the incremental indirect effects). For example, Unilever's Persil lost market leadership in the heavy duty detergent market in the UK to Procter & Gamble's Ariel in the 1980s by being econometrically precisely wrong, rather than judgementally vaguely right. Raj Srivastava's research provides a strong basis on which to understand indirect and carry-over effects.[5] Inputs may either affect current performance (a flow of cash), such as sales, or may build a stock of market-based assets that may be used to generate future cash flows (such as brand equity or a strong customer base).

The second potential danger of metrics is one of diversion. In economics the phenomenon of 'crowding out' occurs when the undertaking of one activity sucks the oxygen from others, giving them no room to exist. One of the exciting aspects of marketing is its combination of logic and intuition. The creativity of marketing has been long acknowledged, as has its impact on generating consumer cut-through. Many market practitioners see a potential conflict between these two forms. We do not see the necessity of a zero-sum approach to marketing, but sensitivity must be exercised to ensure that an increase in measurement and accountability is not accompanied by a change in culture, which values data and analysis and (by implication) does not encourage thinking outside the box with no visible means of support. If a culture of creativity and radical innovation is to be maintained, it must be institutionalised in exactly the same way that is currently being done for measurement and accountability. Luckily we have some good models with which to undertake this activity.

The final potential danger of the new-found emphasis on marketing metrics is also one of omission. A major purpose of marketing metrics systems is to act as a control mechanism to ensure the appropriate levels of inputs to customer-facing activities, planned levels of outputs (both from the perspective of the consumer and the firm) and the efficient transformation between the two. As such, marketing metrics systems have the tendency to be very operationally focused and have a comforting effect on CEOs, analysts and boards. They ensure that the sails of the organisation are well trimmed to take advantage of the current environmental conditions. This tactical focus again has the potential to draw senior decision makers (both within marketing and outside) away from the big problems and issues that are likely to have a much stronger influence on the organisation's future success and market value than many operational ones. This problem is exacerbated by the fact that, as marketers, we really do not have any good metrics to think about the long-term health of the firm and its customer-facing activities.

[5] Srivastava, R., Shervani, T. and Fahey, L. (1998), 'Market-based assets and shareholder value: a framework for analysis', *Journal of Marketing*, 62, 1–14.

EXPERT VOICE

We close with a simple framework that might allow senior managers to think strategically about the marketing future of their organisation, and the actions they need to take to capitalise on the opportunities it offers. We base this on an extension to the Ansoff matrix that classifies opportunities into those springing from new or existing products and from new and existing markets (or customers), as illustrated below:

	Existing brands	New brands	Total brand value
Existing customers	❶ Revenue persistence ❷ Penentration growth	❸ New product development growth	CLV (customer lifetime value) of existing customers
New customers	❹ Market development growth	❺ Diversification growth	Customer acquisition value
Total account value	Current brand equity	New brand equity	Firm value

The strategic challenges facing the firm emerge quite clearly from this matrix. The Hippocratic oath of 'First do no harm' suggests that revenue persistence (1) should be a top priority for established market leaders. Growth may come in terms of getting more out of existing customers in existing markets (2), new brand development (3), customer acquisition (4) and diversification (5). Marketers have good models to understand threats and potential opportunities in each of these areas. Having a framework to unite them enables managers to balance growth between existing and new businesses, to examine the risk profile of the firm in total and to calibrate and harness positive and negative synergies between the firm's different strategic elements.

8

GETTING TO THE TOP

Finally, think about what you need to do to stand out among your peers, stay up to date and get ahead. As you progress up the corporate ladder you need to focus continuously on performance, and increasingly look up and out as opposed to in and down. Your network will be more and more important and you will need to start to think and act like a director.

Focus on performance

Fast Track managers know what is important and what is not, and they have the ability to focus on those key performance indicators (KPIs) that have the greatest impact on what they are trying to achieve. At all times they will understand where they are now, what the bottlenecks are and how to clear them. They recognise the power of learning from past performances and they think ahead to bypass or resolve issues before they become crises. By always delivering against expectations, they stand out from the pack and will always be considered for promotion at the appropriate time.

Performance snapshot: past

There is a universal complaint from historians that politicians don't learn from the lessons of history. This tends to be true of businesses as well. Without a clear understanding of what has happened before, we risk repeating mistakes from the past through inappropriate or ill-judged activity. The review phase of the four-stage marketing process urges teams to assess past performance continually at a tactical and strategic level. How did we perform? How effective was the approach we used and how efficiently did we execute the activity? With hindsight, what could have been done better and what pitfalls would we avoid next time?

This is useful from the team's perspective and also from a wider one. Marketing mistakes are always very visible to the rest of the organisation. Whether these mistakes are a badly received advertising campaign or a poorly chosen marketing slogan, balance any failure by explaining to colleagues how marketing techniques have been used to support them in their work so that they have a stake in any marketing successes. Ingrain this kind of thinking in day-to-day activity and you will keep your team aware of how well you are performing now and in the past, as well as understanding the reasons for that performance.

On its own this approach will only provide lessons learned from your own experiences. To capture organisational learning and performance you need some sort of system. Some organisations maintain a lessons-learned database but these databases are often rarely used. The trouble is that they are easy to set up, but it can be difficult to provide easy access for the right people to find the right information when they need it. If one exists in your business, think about how you would find out information regarding earlier activities.

So, moving on from the distant past to more recent times, keep track of your marketing KPIs, the trends in performance and the notable lessons and issues faced, so that you will be prepared for all questions and opportunities.

QUICK TIP **DIRECT THE JOURNEY**
Current performance is a junction on a journey from where you were to your desired destination. Just as you need to decide to turn left, right or straight on at a crossroads, simply decide whether current performance is Red, Amber or Green, and then take appropriate action.

Performance snapshot: present – current situation (gap)

In order to focus on the right priorities, Fast Track marketing leaders will make sure they keep on top of current performance and that they don't turn problems into crises. That way, they will keep any gap between current and desired performance to a minimum. They will want to know:

→ what is currently going on and what marketing projects are underway;

→ whether or not they are on track;

→ what issues have materialised and who is dealing with them.

Make sure you get this information in a specific way, not as a series of vague intentions. You may consider continuing the use of the SMART acronym by requesting that you want information updates that are specific, measurable, accurate, relevant and timely. Of course, you might also have an ongoing system that helps you and the team keep on top of this.

Performance snapshot: future

The problem with most KPIs – and many other performance measures, including profit and loss accounts – is that they focus on what has just happened. Using them to support activity and decision making today and tomorrow can be a little like driving down the road using nothing but the rear-view mirror. You should check that your marketing KPIs address all three time periods: the present and the future as well as the past. You obviously can't measure the outputs on forward-facing KPIs but you can make sure you are taking steps that help to ensure the future health of the business. Part of that is to make sure the pipeline of marketing activity is still aligned to the current business imperatives, as these will often change throughout the year.

Think about risks and risk management. You need an understanding of which activities are likely to be successful and which will fail so that you can be ready to deal with the casualties. Whether these are market offerings, products or product lines, campaigns or just one-off projects, you should try to get early indications of problems so that you can either take remedial action or ensure that the activity is retired gracefully.

Many innovative technology companies, whether in mobile phones, gaming or IT, track what percentage of revenue is made up of newly released products. This is important to demonstrate the return on R&D and to support an innovative, leadership market position. But these companies also expect a wide range of success levels. Obviously lots of ideas, even after significant investment, get canned before release to the market, while some might get test-marketed and then dropped. Some are withdrawn shortly after release for a whole host of reasons, while others go on to deliver strong profit for years to come. The trick is in managing the portfolio, whether activities or products, and taking early action to maintain momentum.

In summary, think ahead, plan ahead and stay ahead.

Invite challenge

Who can we get to challenge us?

Fast Track managers never rest on their laurels. You may think that your performance is on track, but as the external business environment changes you need to adapt. Look for ways to introduce challenge for yourself and your team on a regular basis. This can be to refine strategies and messages, or to bring in new ideas, tools or processes. Make sure you seek challenge from a variety of audiences, both internal and external. Some groups are more radical and direct than others, and so it is worth reviewing the following:

→ **Internal teams**. These may include sales teams, finance and senior management. There are sure to be a few marketing sceptics in there, so get their views and see whether you can convince them of your direction, but also see whether you can use their feedback and comment.

→ **Customers**. How are their must-haves, needs and wants changing? What future scenarios might occur? Make sure you don't just talk to the 'friendlies', the ones that we know like us. Talk to a cross-section of new, old, big and small.

→ **Competitors**. How can we learn from them? What are they doing now that could be copied ('swiped')?

→ **Partners**. Again, they will always have an agenda, but they can provide some very valuable input, so what can we learn from them? Are they getting different inputs from the market than you? Have they spotted a new customer-buying pattern or are they aware of competitive promotions in the pipeline?

→ **Influencers**. What are the 'experts' recommending to the market? These might be industry analysts or even the press. Don't always spend your time with these people trying to sell – it can often be just as important to listen. By talking to them in the appropriate circumstances about what you are doing and your market proposition, you will get a lot of valuable feedback.

Engage in challenging acts on a regular basis, even if you are meeting your KPIs because you're ahead of the game. If you are finding it easy to meet the targets set for you, then don't wait for your boss to make them more stretching, do it yourself. Perhaps take time to get involved in areas where you are not so confident in order to develop yourself. Remember to use relevant opportunities for self-development, both inside and outside work.

How do I keep up to date?

As well as working with other groups inside and outside of the business, think carefully about what additional sources of knowledge and insight you want to receive and how often. There is a wealth of information available from a variety of sources, so you need to be selective, as the time you have available for reading is limited.

→ **Web**. This provides a huge variety of free and subscription information from many sources. The trick is to harness the power and scope of the information on the web without getting distracted and unfocused. *Fast Track recommendation: review the websites of your 'top ten' customers and competitors at least twice a year and identify up to five other useful websites that provide challenge. Also consider tools such as RSS feeds to push relevant information to you, as well as key aggregation sites.*

→ **Publications**. Journals, magazines and papers are often available via subscription. These contain the latest ideas and thinking available, but unfortunately also contain a lot of commercial advertorials. *Fast Track recommendation: subscribe to the one journal of greatest relevance to your industry for one year and review its value. Once you have read it, make sure you circulate it to other members of your team.*

→ **Conferences**. These provide a useful opportunity to listen to other perspectives and are typically an excellent way of networking with others outside the business, but they can be time consuming and expensive. *Fast Track recommendation: identify the one conference of greatest relevance and attend it for two consecutive years. Aim to identify at least three people (other attendees or presenters) to follow up with about specific issues you have.*

→ **Online communities**. There are many online discussion forums between like-minded or peer groups within the marketing community. *Fast Track recommendation: these can be extremely useful or a complete waste of time, so give them a go and see what value you get.*

→ **Benchmarking**. Whether done in a structured and formal manner or informally via key network contacts, this is a valuable way of identifying new ideas and approaches and stretching the way you think, although it does take a certain amount of effort to set up and manage. *Fast Track recommendation: definitely worth doing, so perhaps identify two or three other organisations that you respect and admire, and meet them up to four times a year. You might feel it best to use a facilitator and follow a structured agenda to maximise the cross-company learning. Remember that you will have to give value to them as well as the other way round.*

→ **Professional bodies**. Membership of these bodies, such as the Chartered Institute of Marketing (CIM) or the Institute of Directors (IoD), becomes more important the more senior you become, and is often a source of free advice. *Fast Track recommendation: once you have been in your role for at least a year, sign up for a year and see what benefits you receive.*

Fast-Track-Me.com. All the key ideas, tools and techniques contained in the Fast Track series are available via the internet at **www.Fast-Track-Me.com**. *Fast Track recommendation: first, allocate 30 minutes to visit and explore the site. It contains a rich source of tips, tools and techniques, stories, expert voices and online audits from the Fast Track series.*

Remember that whatever your source of information, to maximise the benefits you need to put time aside and make the necessary effort. However, also recognise that you will never have perfect knowledge – particularly as marketing is ultimately dealing with and influencing future market and human behaviours. Decide what level of certainty will be good enough and then act on it. Remember, as the figure below shows, seeking information and removing uncertainties becomes more expensive until, for example, the last 2 per cent is prohibitively expensive.

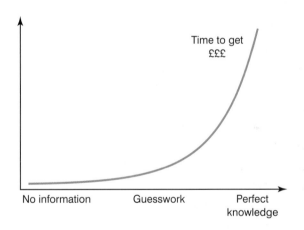

Getting promoted

The Fast Track manager will seek to identify appropriate promotion opportunities. This may occur within a few months or possibly a number of years, but in either case take time to reflect on your state of readiness. Identify the future role you are keen to fulfil and clarify the criteria you will need to satisfy in terms of skills, experience, attitudes and behaviours. Ask yourself the following questions:

→ **Capability**. Do I have what it takes? What have I achieved and learned so far?

→ **Credibility**. Can I demonstrate and convince others that I can and will perform well in the role?

→ **Desire**. Do I want the role and do I have sufficient drive and enthusiasm to do a great job?

→ **Relationships**. Do I have positive working relationships with the right people?

→ **Competitive**. What would make me the most appropriate candidate, given all the alternatives?

If you have concerns, then put in place a plan to address them. Timing is the key, so make sure you are well prepared before putting yourself forward for the role.

If you are seeking a promotion within the business as opposed to stepping outside, you also need to consider the relationship that you have with your peers and how that is likely to change with a promotion. People who were peers and colleagues could well end up working for you. In preparing yourself for promotion bear this in mind and establish your leadership credentials early, based on respect, expert authority and a positive mindset. In other words, demonstrate to your peers that you are the best person for the job and you deserve the role. This reduces any chance of 'sour grapes' from other team members. Of course, when you get the promotion you then need to work hard to develop those leadership qualities and bring the team along with you.

 CASE STORY *TECHNOLOGY INDUSTRY, IAN'S STORY*

Narrator Ian is a senior marketing manager responsible for a number of products and markets for a global software company.

Context Ian had spent his whole career in the technology sector, working for large corporates, tech start-ups and marketing agencies.

Issue After steady and consistent progression in marketing and product marketing roles, the rate of Ian's career development started to slow. Obviously things can slow down as people get older and opportunities become fewer, but Ian wanted to keep up the pace of his development from both a career and a capability perspective.

Solution Ian focused on a few key areas. He made sure he was keeping up to date and learning from the latest thinking by attending targeted courses and conferences and joining professional bodies, including the Chartered Institute of Marketing and the Institute of Directors. He also put more effort into networking and keeping in contact with peers and colleagues, which was made easier with modern internet technology.

Learning Ian decided to look beyond his day-to-day job and make an effort to combine it with the three elements of continual learning, professional development and peer networking. By doing so, he was able to accelerate his career path and reach his goals.

Becoming a director

How do I get to the top?

Ask yourself, 'Do I really want to get to the top?' In our early careers we often believe that this should be our natural goal, but for many people the price is too much to pay. While the personal and financial rewards can be high, many people do not enjoy the additional responsibilities, stress and pressures on their work–life balance that are generally associated with getting to the top.

It is very important to answer this question very honestly. The natural, instinctive and immediate reaction is to say, 'Yes, of course I want the top job!' – but have you really thought about it? What is driving you to that response? It might be the money, or the power and status, or the belief that you can make a difference. A colleague, who was a regional managing director for a US technology company, once said to me that, 'The higher you climb the corporate ladder, the thinner the oxygen gets, while the view doesn't really get any better.' There might be all sorts of other things going on in your life, so there is nothing wrong with deciding that you have got to where you want for the time being.

Take time to get to know the other directors in the business, as well as the marketing director. What do they do on a day-to-day basis and what do they need to achieve for success? What are the pressures and the risks? Recognise that the more senior you get, the lonelier the position is likely to be, as you end up with fewer and fewer peers. It is often said that the role of the chief executive is the loneliest one in the business.

QUICK TIP *IDENTIFY YOUR BALANCE*
Only you can decide how you want to balance your life and work. While we all accept that there will be periods when that balance shifts and comes under pressure, make a conscious decision as to the balance you want and review it every so often to check it's still in line with reality.

On the other hand, getting to the top in marketing can be one of the most rewarding and enjoyable jobs of the lot. So if you want it, go for it. Make sure you understand what criteria senior managers use to assess potential candidates for the job. Don't leave this too late, as it may take you a few years to acquire the necessary experience and demonstrate that you have the skills.

What will my responsibilities be?

As well as heading up marketing activities throughout the business, you might have certain roles and statutory responsibilities that accompany the title of director. Depending on your business, you might be designated as an official company director and have a seat on the board of directors, or you might be a director in name only, which simply signifies your seniority in the business. Either way, the title means that you are likely to be involved in:

→ determining the company's strategic objectives and policies;

→ monitoring progress towards achieving the objectives and policies;

→ appointing the senior management team;

→ accounting for the company's activities to relevant parties, e.g. shareholders;

→ attending board meetings that run the company, with the high level of integrity that is inferred by statutory standards and the company's interpretation of corporate governance, particularly in sensitive areas such as health and safety.

You will also have to conduct yourself in a highly professional manner.

→ A director must not put themselves in a position where the interests of the company conflict with their personal interest or their duty to a third party.

→ A director must not make a personal profit out of their position as a director unless they are permitted to do so by the company.

→ A director must act in a bona fide manner when dealing with the interests of the company as a whole, ensuring that no other purpose or agenda impacts decisions or activities.

Planning your exit strategy

At some stage you will want to change role. You may be moving on, getting your boss's job or even retiring early, but whatever the situation the way you manage the transition is critical to sustaining the performance of your team. Take time to plan the last ten weeks in your current role to the same level of detail as you did the first ten weeks, ensuring that your successor is well prepared and excited about taking on their new role.

What is succession planning?

Once you have fully settled into your role you should start to think about who might be your natural replacement. Remember that it may take at least two years to develop their skills and experience. There may be more than one internal candidate, or it may be that none will meet the criteria, but in either case your succession is important and you need to plan it in advance for the sake of the business.

Handover tips

At the point of transition, manage the handover to your successor effectively, ensuring that you transfer information and relationships smoothly. Use the checklist in Chapter 6 (page 123) as a structure for preparing your handover document. Then focus on people and key relationships, taking time to introduce your successor face to face rather than simply sending around an email. Take time to reflect on your original vision and how well you achieved it, then capture a list of lessons learned and add it to your handover notes.

STOP – THINK – ACT

In this final chapter you will have identified what you need to do to get to the top. How is marketing represented at the highest levels in your current organisation? Hopefully you will have a marketing voice at board level, perhaps with the title of chief marketing officer (CMO). If marketing is simply tagged on to the end of the sales director's title, then that might give you a different indication of how marketing is perceived in the company.

Stop and reflect on your career aspirations – what do you want to be doing in three years' time?

My vision	What do I want to be doing in three years' time?
My supporters	Whose support will I need to get there?
My capabilities	What capabilities and experience will I need to succeed?
My progress	What milestones will I achieve along the way?

Visit www.Fast-Track-Me.com to use the Fast Track online planning tool.

Marketers must step up to the mark

Paul Gostick

There is a clear paradox in how organisations perceive marketing. On the one hand, nearly every CEO puts marketing at the top of the agenda, and rightly so. A market orientation that focuses on disciplines and processes, creates value, enables the company to gain a real understanding of customers and finally meet their needs profitably is the essential foundation for building a world-class company. Conversely, many marketing professionals and departments are undervalued by senior managers in other functions. Few chief executives are from a marketing background, few marketing directors are on the board and professional qualifications are not taken seriously. Yet the very philosophy of marketing is seen as essential to the business.

The problem is that most strategic marketing proposals tend to focus on advertising, communication, lead generation and the like, and are measured in bland, nebulous terms such as increasing awareness, market share or sales volume. Marketing teams rarely see the need to link marketing spend to the impact on the bottom line and the financial value of the business. In today's economic climate there is tremendous pressure on senior managers to deliver shareholder value and it is therefore inevitable that marketing's voice is weakened in such circumstances and that marketers are viewed as a cost rather than an investment. To illustrate the point, which budget gets cut first in an economic downturn?

It seems that marketing isn't working well today. New products are failing at an alarming rate. Many advertising campaigns fail to register anything distinctive in customers' minds. Direct mail typically achieves a 1–2 per cent response rate and we accept this as the norm. What we don't know or understand is what impact such communication has had on the 98–99 per cent that didn't respond. E-marketing, although immediate, tailorable, quickly changed and relatively low cost, is becoming intrusive. Many products are perceived as interchangeable commodities rather than as powerful brands and therefore fall prey to low prices and undifferentiated propositions. Innovation is limited to minor product or service enhancements or extensions rather than a real step-change. The old tag of marketing being a 'promotions tool' lingers on.

Engineering-led companies tend to make things and then spend a fortune trying to sell them to prospective customers, usually with little success

EXPERT VOICE

because they have not understood the market or customers' needs. There are countless business organisations that feel quite safe in restricting the role of their marketing department to one of a sales support function. Individuals working in such departments often find themselves on the receiving end of a never-ending stream of promotional requests from other areas of the business.

In B2B markets segmentation is typically crude, focusing on firmographics – size, location, sector, etc. Rarely does the segmentation focus on motivators – why do customers buy? Ultimately, purchase decisions are emotional not rational, which is why motivators are so critical. In the final analysis, rational decisions lead to conclusions, but emotional decisions lead to actions. Actions lead to sales and business.

Marketers must protect and enhance their marketing assets, many of which are intangible and thus a foundation for differentiation. Today's customers are time poor and information rich. They expect better service, lower prices, higher quality and more value. Channels and routes to market are proliferating and consolidating. Competition comes from all over the world, thanks to rapid developments in communications technology, available bandwidth and the World Wide Web.

Not surprisingly, there is a call for a reinvention of marketing. Marketing should be at the heart of the business and driving the strategic agenda. Until there is a sea change in attitudes, marketers will continue to focus on tactical communication and lead-generation activity, and will be seen as a cost – unaccountable and expendable.

As management guru Peter Drucker said almost 50 years ago, 'The purpose of a company is to create a customer … The only profit centre is the customer … The business has two, and only two, basic functions – marketing and innovation. Marketing and innovation produce results: all the rest are costs.' Drucker's claim is no less true today.

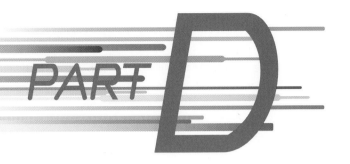

PART D

DIRECTOR'S
TOOLKIT

In Part B we introduced ten core tools and techniques that can be used from day one in your new role as a team leader or manager in your chosen field. As you progress up the career ladder to the role of senior manager, and as your team matures in terms of their understanding and capabilities, you will want to introduce more advanced or sophisticated techniques.

Part D provides a number of more comprehensive tools, techniques and frameworks developed and adopted by industry leaders – helping you to differentiate from your competitors.

	TOOL DESCRIPTION
T1	Team marketing audit
T2	Integrated marketing plans
T3	Market analysis
T4	Analysis tools
T5	Marketing project checklist

T1 TEAM
MARKETING AUDIT

Use the following checklist[1] to assess the current state of your team. Consider each criterion in turn and use the following scoring system to identify current performance:

0 Not done or defined within the business: unaware of its importance to marketing management

1 Aware of area but little or no work done in the business

2 Recognised as an area of importance and some work done in this area

3 Area clearly defined and work done in the area in terms of marketing management

4 Consistent use of best practice tools and techniques in this area across the business

5 Area recognised as being 'best in class' and could be a reference area for best practice

Reflect on the lowest scores and identify those areas that are critical to success and flag them as status Red, requiring immediate attention. Then identify those areas that you are concerned about and flag those as status Amber, implying areas of risk that need to be monitored closely. Status Green implies that you are happy with the current state.

---

[1] Integrated Marketing Framework, Sine Qua Non International Ltd, 2008.

ID	CATEGORY	EVALUATION CRITERIA	SCORE	STATUS
M1	**Basic principles**		**0–5**	**RAG**
A	Market focus	The organisation is focused on identifying and meeting the needs of clearly defined markets of accessible customers		
B	USP	The company and its products/services are clearly differentiated in the marketplace with a clear and succinct unique selling proposition (USP)		
C	Alignment	Marketing is aligned with all functions to ensure that markets and customers actually experience the differentiated proposition promised by the brand(s)		
M2	**Strategic marketing**			
A	Life cycle management	Market cycles and associated behaviours are understood and products are managed proactively through each stage		
B	Portfolio management	Brands and products are actively managed as portfolios, recognising and harnessing the 360-degree SWOT position of the individual elements and the whole		
C	Segmentation	High-growth and high-emphasis segments are identified using tools, including a product-market matrix		
M3	**Marketing mix**			
A	The four Ps	The four Ps, reflecting price, product, promotion and placement, are defined for all key products and service offerings		
B	Competitive positioning	The market is constantly monitored in terms of positioning and competitor activity and the marketing mix is adjusted accordingly		
C	Sales alignment	Mix elements, in particular promotions and sales channels, are aligned to optimise the impact of marketing on key business imperatives		

ID	CATEGORY	EVALUATION CRITERIA	SCORE	STATUS
M4	**Extended marketing mix**		0–5	RAG
A	More Ps and a few Rs	All opportunities and tools to differentiate marketing and to develop relevance, relationships, responsiveness and receptivity are explored and understood	☐	☐
B	Integration	All mix elements are exercised and integrated as appropriate, to maximise the effectiveness and return of activities	☐	☐
C	Customer experience and advocacy	The whole end-to-end customer experience is identified, mapped, monitored and managed, to the extent that customers will willingly recommend you and your offering to others	☐	☐
M5	**Digital marketing**			
A	Scanning	Developments and trends in new media, information access and digital technologies are constantly monitored and evaluated in terms of their potential to engage with target markets	☐	☐
B	Blending	Messages are tuned to the medium, based on an understanding of customer behaviours and preferences	☐	☐
C	Consistency	Brand consistency is maintained across all channels and activities are integrated and audited to maximum return and legislatory compliance	☐	☐
M6	**Marketing management – understand**			
A	Business context	All marketing activities have clear goals and objectives and are aligned to one or more business imperative	☐	☐
B	External environment	Specific target customer musts and wants are understood and drive local marketing planning	☐	☐
C	Barriers	Resources and constraints, internal and external, that are critical to success are identified and managed accordingly	☐	☐

ID	CATEGORY	EVALUATION CRITERIA	SCORE	STATUS
M7	**Marketing management – develop**		0–5	RAG
A	Marketing plan	Marketing plans are created to support product-market initiatives in line with the marketing strategy and mix		
B	Creative solutions	A process exists for challenging the status quo and generating 'breakthrough' ideas		
C	Stakeholder engagement	Key stakeholders are engaged and committed to marketing strategies and plans		
M8	**Marketing management – execute**			
A	Tasks and timing	Project and programme management discipline and tools exist to ensure the effective and efficient delivery of marketing activity		
B	Commitment to excellence	All team members demonstrate a commitment to excellence and/or brand values in delivering marketing activity		
C	Risk management	Project and programme issues and risks, including the external environment, are actively and routinely managed by marketing teams		
M9	**Marketing management – review**			
A	Early indicators	All activities are tracked from inception, to ensure on-target delivery		
B	Re-evaluation	Project and programme outcomes are evaluated in terms of the effectiveness of the strategy in achieving goals and objectives		
C	Insights and learnings	All insights and learnings from projects and programmes are captured and fed back into future strategies and plans		

ID	CATEGORY	EVALUATION CRITERIA	SCORE	STATUS
M10	Performance management – evaluation, metrics and returns		0–5	RAG
A	Marketing KPIs	All activities are managed against SMART objectives, which in turn relate back to marketing key performance indicators	☐	☐
B	Performance reviews	A framework exists to review and evaluate the performance and impact of marketing overall	☐	☐
C	ROMI	Return on marketing investment is tracked in terms of financial indicators as well as performance against key objectives	☐	☐

For each element of the checklist add up the scores of the three related questions and divide by three – this will give you an average score for that specific element. Here is an example:

ELEMENT	SCORE	0	1	2	3	4	5	NOTES
Basic principles	2.1			■				
Strategic marketing	4.2					■		Clear vision and market understanding
Marketing mix	3.6				■			Strong product and promotion, weak with channel
Extended marketing mix	4.6					■		Good relationship development and experiential marketing
Digital marketing	1.2		■					Weak on vision and implementation
Marketing management – understand	2.6			■				
Marketing management – develop	1.7		■					Strategy selection and stakeholder buy-in?
Marketing management – execute	4.6					■		Strong action orientation
Marketing management – review	4.4					■		Good project measurement
Performance management	3.8				■			

With an integrated framework the whole marketing process is only as strong as the weakest of the individual elements. If one 'link in the chain' is weak then the marketing function and activity within the company will not operate to optimum efficiency and there is an increased risk of failure. The action plan, therefore, should be to focus attention and resources on the elements of greatest weakness first, and then to move the whole framework to a level of excellence. This approach optimises the use of resources and sets up a process of continuous improvement.

In the example above, the managers conducting the marketing audit have identified that the weakest link is that of the *digital marketing* (average score 1.2). The plan would therefore be to focus attention on and improve the use of digital marketing to strengthen market position until it was no longer the weakest link. This could be achieved by exploring new digital strategies, altering the balance of various media and testing how audiences respond. Once the senior management team has increased confidence that digital marketing has improved, the next stage would be to focus on *marketing management – develop* (scoring 1.7), to think more about strategic options, planning and getting stakeholder buy-in, before jumping into action. Only then should you look to strengthen *basic principles* (which scored 2.1).

T2 INTEGRATED MARKETING PLANS

What are plans for?

Teams talk of preparing marketing plans and people nod their heads in agreement, but in fact there is very little common understanding of what a marketing plan consists of. There are some consistent areas: probably 80–90 per cent of plans would include a SWOT analysis. But without being overly prescriptive, it is important that there is a shared understanding of what a plan is and the reasons people are putting one together.

Part of the confusion arises from a lack of clarity of purpose and timescale. Businesses actually need different plans for different purposes. The renowned marketing planning guru, Professor Malcolm McDonald, advocates two levels of plan: one at the strategic level for the business unit; and a tactical, one-year, short-term plan. Too often people either try to combine these two into one or simply ignore the strategic plan. They either believe that someone else, probably in headquarters, is looking after the strategic plan, or think that the market is changing so fast it's difficult to have a long-term perspective on it. In many organisations facing pressure from stock markets for performance on a quarterly basis, the one-year plan is the strategic plan, because things will have changed significantly both internally and externally by the end of the year.

This possibly explains the philosophy seen during many planning cycles. Get the plan completed and kick off the key activities, and then consign the plan to a folder somewhere to be looked at again in six or nine or even twelve months' time. This means that a lot of time and effort is in effect wasted on putting plans together that are rarely actively used. If we take a different perspective, the whole activity can and should create more value.

→ **A strategic marketing plan.** This plan should have a rolling medium- to long-term window of between two and five years, although this is typically three. This sets the marketing direction for the business, at whatever level the business is operating: it could be a UK territory plan or a plan for a product division. The plan identifies the characteristics of the markets that the business is in and wishes to operate in, the basis of competitive advantage and differentiation, and a summary of the portfolio of offerings presented to the market. Marketing objectives are clearly stated and broken down and strategies and resources are outlined for achieving these objectives.

→ **A tactical plan.** While incorporating some similar terminology, this plan is much more focused on what implementation activities are taking place when, to actually deliver on key objectives. Covering a period of anything from three months to a year, the tactical plan tends to centre on outbound activities that deliver the various marketing mix elements to customers, prospects and influencers.

Barriers to effective planning

While most people accept the need for marketing planning, there are still some barriers to effective planning that teams need to overcome. There is a certain amount of confusion in a number of areas: between the different types of plan described above and also between marketing objectives, strategies and tactics.

Prioritisation can also be difficult. Less is more sounds a great philosophy but in practice marketing managers find it difficult to leave things out. These plans should be just as specific in terms of what opportunities you will *not* be addressing.

A real issue is often either the lack of the reliable, accurate data on which to base decisions and plans, or a lack of analysis on that data to draw valid conclusions. Make sure you don't let your team fall into the trap of filling in the gaps in understanding with guesswork and assumptions. The quality of the output, in terms of the plan and the activities being driven by the plan, can only be as good as the inputs and information that go in. The old adage 'garbage in, garbage out' holds true for marketing planning as well as computer systems.

Plan templates

Here are sample templates for a strategic marketing plan and a tactical plan.

Strategic marketing plan template[1]

→ **Mission and boundary statements**. Outline the vision that you and the stakeholders are working towards and provide an explicit statement of the boundaries that are implicit in that vision.

→ **Financial summary**. Summarise the key current financial numbers that the plan is looking to impact.

→ **Market overview**. Review the market trends and structure, highlighting key segments and maturity cycles. Tools used here should include gap analysis, life cycle analysis and the extended Ansoff box.

→ **Portfolio summary**. Map out the market and product portfolios for the business, using tools such as the BCG/GE matrix.

→ **Opportunities and threats**. Following a thorough analysis of the market, identify opportunities and threats for the overall market but also break these down by market segment, product or portfolio group.

[1] Adapted from McDonald, Malcolm (2007), *Marketing Plans: How to Prepare Them, How to Use Them*, Oxford: Butterworth Heinemann. Reproduced with permission.

→ **Strengths and weaknesses.** Again following an internal audit, identify overall strengths and weaknesses as well as a more detailed breakdown by segment and product line.

→ **Issues to address.** Outline the issues and opportunities arising from the SWOT that need to be addressed, either as part of the plan or by the business in a wider context. Identify issues' owners and a timeline.

→ **Assumptions.** Clearly state the assumptions and risks that the plan is based upon, such as continued market growth rates, economic forecasts and competitor activity.

→ **Marketing objectives.** Set out marketing objectives by explicitly defining strategic focus and portfolio composition (including areas for development, deletion, extension) for both products and markets.

→ **Marketing strategies.** Outline the key strategies, including positioning, for both the overall thrust and for various portfolio elements.

→ **Resource requirements.** Provide an outline of the resources and budget required to achieve the marketing objectives through the implementation of the identified strategies.

Tactical marketing plan template[2]

→ **Executive summary.** Where are we now? Where do we want to be? How do we plan to get there?

→ **Statement of purpose.** An outline of what the plan and associated activities are aiming to achieve (such as a 20 per cent increase in sales in the 'take home' beer market or closer relationships with key customers in the pharmaceutical sector). What are the objectives?

→ **Baseline performance.** Where we are starting from in terms of performance and, if appropriate, what activities have got us to that position.

[2] Sine Qua Non International Ltd, 2008.

→ **SWOT**. The usual format for a SWOT, again best constructed as an OTSW as in the strategic plan, but this time addressing the specifics of this situation, opportunity or market.

→ **Marketing strategy and activity**. How you aim to achieve the objectives stated. What activity will you undertake? Does the tactical marketing activity align with the wider strategic view and plan?

→ **Forecast and budget**. The resources, budgets and forecast milestones.

→ **Implementation timeline**. A detailed timeline of activities, from project inception through to completion and review.

→ **Assumptions, risks and controls**. What assumptions are incorporated in the plan, both internally and externally? What risks have been identified and what plans are in place to mitigate them? What controls in terms of project check points are established to ensure successful delivery? In other words, how will you know if and when you start to lose your way for whatever reason? (For example, the market or the economic climate might change to such an extent that target customers spend less money or a key partner or supplier gets distracted and lets you down.)

→ **Appendices**. Any supporting data, including market or customer information.

Why does marketing need to be integrated?

Since marketing in its true sense is so vital to the business, so is taking an integrated approach to its management. A clear and effective business and marketing strategy combined with efficient marketing tactics and operations will maximise the chances that you, your team, marketing and, in turn, the business will thrive. The alternatives are less palatable but can be redeemed with the right action. But the right effort up front in terms of strategic thinking, together with the right planning and execution of activities, should help to make sure you stay in the green box in the figure overleaf.

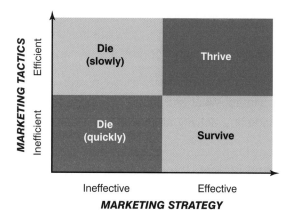

Integrated marketing means that the business has a consistent and coordinated approach to markets and customers. This is at both the strategic level and the tactical level. For large organisations a chief marketing officer (CMO) should report to the CEO and possibly the board, with an aligned and integrated view of the various divisions, business units and groups – or whatever structure is used in the business. While many large businesses have the role, only a proportion take marketing seriously enough to have board-level representation.

In a smaller business it is still key that the marketing or sales and marketing director, or even the CEO, has a picture of how the various marketing activities link together to make a whole. Even though the tactical activities will be addressing different market opportunities, they should still be aligned and consistent and should avoid conflicting with each other.

Only by using an appropriate variety of tools and techniques and continuously monitoring inputs and outputs of the marketing process will management understand the benefits of marketing. It is now recognised that marketing is part management science and process, part analysis and knowledge, and part creativity. Only by linking those elements together through an integrated framework can marketing hope to maximise its impact on the business.

T3 MARKET ANALYSIS

The importance of knowledge

Why does marketing depend on the capture of data and the accessibility of information?

Although marketing plan cycles might suggest that key decisions are taken at set times during the year, marketing teams and business leaders are in fact constantly assessing and making choices about marketing, markets and competitors. From the board making strategic choices in terms of new market opportunities and investments, to marketing team leaders responding to competitor promotions, this happens at all levels.

All these decisions need to be based on accurate information that provides the context and the pertinent facts. Without the facts, decision making relies too heavily on intuition or instinct, and in many situations this is not sufficient. Intuition improves with experience, but for the new manager it is all too easy to make gut-feel mistakes. We don't live in a perfect world, so we generally don't have access to all the information we would like, but we should still seek data-driven decisions where possible. Too often fancy terminology and jargon is used to explain situations or decisions, but in reality everyone knows that while some good information was available, some aspects may be little more than guesswork.

Marketing is concerned with customer behaviours both now and in the future, so that makes it difficult to forecast. However, don't underestimate the importance of gathering data on a continuous basis and making it accessible to people engaged in marketing thinking.

So what information is required?

By now we should all recognise that marketing requires a lot more than telling the world about your great products and building your market share. A prolonged period of that kind of approach could simply end with you in an utterly dominant position as the market-share leader in black and white televisions.

You need to be looking at trends and developments in the internal and external environments. Innovative R&D from you or a competitor might have uncovered a new technology that will transform the market or create a parallel market. Even customers themselves often don't know what their future needs and spending are likely to be.

The rate and extent of change in your industry, and the business context in which you are working, will to a large extent determine the requirement for information. However, we can define key categories of information as a checklist to make sure that we gather the most appropriate information to feed into the marketing process and decision making.

Market scanning

Without a good understanding of what is happening in the industry or market in which we compete, we run the risk of missing exciting new markets, or failing to see threats until it is too late to respond. Trends in the external environment present both opportunities and threats, but in both cases there may be situations requiring innovative solutions to stay ahead. By accepting that many new ideas will originate outside the organisation we can keep track of trends and opportunities and assess when we should adopt and address them.

Market opportunities are driven in one way or another by evolutionary trends or discontinuities in the industry in which we operate. Discontinuities occur when something creates a dramatic change in the business context, such as a breakthrough in technology. Examples would be the change from cathode ray tube TVs to plasma and LCD flat screen TVs, to the emerging OLED TV, and from vinyl records to CDs to MP3.

The initial market scan should follow the PESTEL model, tracking political changes, economic and social trends, technological discontinuities, as well as environmental trends and legal changes.

Political changes

A change in government or the introduction of new policies will impact many aspects of the economy. It will also result in levels of uncertainty and make organisations more or less willing to invest in new ventures. For example:

→ Government fiscal policy directly affects consumer and business spending.

→ Public sector investment often signals a huge opportunity for the private sector. For instance, health and education spending by the Labour government from the late 1990s onwards.

Economic trends

International exchange rates, rates of inflation or even changes in tax regimes will affect disposable incomes and therefore consumer (and business) spending. For example:

→ In tight economic times business discretionary spend gets slashed. Service providers such as marketing and training are often very hard hit, and so they need to drive costs down and demonstrate strong return on investment.

→ As interest rates come down, the cost of borrowing goes down. Financial services organisations innovate to introduce new forms of borrowing and ways of restructuring corporate debt.

Social trends

Changes in demographics, such as an ageing population, immigration and emigration or movement into or out of towns, will fundamentally change patterns of buying behaviour. For example:

→ **Consumer buying habits are changing as more people are using the internet to buy online.** Traditional retailers have had to innovate to change the way they market to and service this new segment.

→ **Improvements in healthcare have resulted in people living longer and having more active lives.** The 'grey market' or 'silver surfers' represent a significant segment, with disposable income that they often wish to spend on making the most of life for themselves or their children and grandchildren.

Technology discontinuities

Perhaps the biggest external driver for many organisations in recent years has been the relentless developments in all aspects of technology, such as the internet and mobile telephony. For example:

→ **The internet has allowed small and medium-sized enterprises (SMEs) to compete head to head with global companies.** This has often resulted in them aggressively taking market share in the most profitable niches.

→ **The advent of digital media and the internet has transformed the music, entertainment and broadcast industries.** This has opened up new opportunities while at the same time creating issues around copyright and sharing.

Environmental trends

Consideration and care for the environment is getting unprecedented press at present, covering issues ranging from global warming and recycling to working with third world countries. For example:

→ **Genetically modified (GM) crops.** These offer enormous potential to produce more for less, but future legislation and many of the arguments put by each side are still unclear.

→ **Global warming.** This is changing the way tourists take their holidays and the way car manufacturers design and build their cars. Some of these aspects will be regulated, but some will be affected by consumer pressure.

Legal changes

Most Western organisations complain bitterly about the increasing number of laws and regulations they need to comply with. Following recent corporate failures, new standards are being adopted, such as Sarbanes-Oxley. This is a new standard for monitoring and reporting on the business that arose out of corporate failures in the USA, but ultimately impacted all European companies dealing with American businesses. Other examples of legal changes include:

→ **Health and safety regulations**. These might impact on how a product is used in the workplace.

→ **Consumer and data protection laws**. These dictate new buyers' rights and how businesses are required to disclose and hold data about customers and prospects.

Customer and competitor scanning

Without a good understanding of customers and competitors we run the risk of producing products and services that simply will not sell, either because customers don't want them or because they can get them better, cheaper or faster elsewhere. Remember what is important when gathering information about customers and competitors. You need to know what you are offering to your customers and, more importantly, their perception of what you are offering them. The same is true with competitors: find out how their customers perceive their products and services, as well as what they actually are. The 'So what?' test is useful here. If a competitor has a feature that you do not have, make sure it is significant either to their market share or to their customer satisfaction score before taking it as a must-have for your product. Similarly, don't let the fact that you have a unique feature make you think that you automatically have a competitive advantage. Look for information that tells you that customers will want such a feature in the future. (See also the customer value tool in the analysis toolkit on page 191.)

Consider the thinking of Michael Porter and his renowned five forces model.[1] Porter suggested that five forces are at work within any industry:

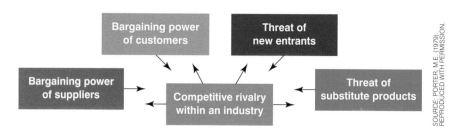

SOURCE: PORTER, M.E. (1979), REPRODUCED WITH PERMISSION.

The balance of these forces sets out the competitive landscape. While all the forces will ultimately impact marketing and the business, three forces are of particular interest to marketers: customers, competitors and substitutes and alternatives.

Customers

Changes in customer must-haves and wants will fundamentally change what it is we do or how we do it, so we need to listen to them and get their feedback. But this is more difficult than it looks, since customer satisfaction surveys – a commonly used tool – are not necessarily good predictors of future purchasing behaviours. Too often companies score 9 out of 10 on a survey and then lose the next contract because of a change in the customer environment that has altered customers' requirements. Remember that you are gathering data about the future, not just about the past.

We need to understand how customers' requirements are changing, what is now most important to them and what their biggest concerns are. Dig around, question and understand how you can use your capabilities to provide exciting new solutions. For example, using focus groups to conduct market research, First Direct identified a significant group of customers that were increasingly comfortable with new technologies. They capitalised on this trend and launched the UK's first telephone banking service, and have stayed at the forefront of technology developments with the advent of internet banking.

[1] Porter, M.E. (1979), 'How competitive forces shape strategy', *Harvard Business Review*, March/April.

Competitors

When looking at customer must-haves and wants it is not enough to understand how we perform. We need to identify how we perform against the competition – what are our strengths and weaknesses? Where have we got an advantage that we can exploit, and where have we got weaknesses that we need to address?

Analysis of competitors needs to be more than a simple cursory review of their financials (balance sheets and profit and loss statements). Think also about background information, what products and services they offer and to which customers and markets, what facilities they have and how good their team is. Perhaps of most interest is to try to predict what their future strategies will be from the directions that are apparent. This could give you a clue about where to protect your current advantages and where to take action should they be exposed.

Develop a thorough 360-degree SWOT for each major competitor, which can then be reviewed and updated as developments and changes occur.

Substitutes and alternatives

And you're not finished yet: start thinking outside the box. So your customers like what you are offering and your competitors appear at a disadvantage – where else might you face a threat? Perhaps someone is approaching from your blindside as you read this: there are people in other industries, possibly so different from yours that you've never even thought of them as competitors, who may be looking at opportunities to present new solutions to your customers' problems. It could be changes in technology, an ability to apply processes, assets and resources to similar but new opportunities, or PESTEL changes that allow them to compete at attractive price points. For example:

→ The major airlines spent a lot of time coming up with innovative ideas for fending off the threat from American airlines and other so-called flag carriers, and completely missed the threat from new low-cost **alternatives** such as easyJet and Ryanair.

→ Similarly, when times are hard airlines know that businesspeople will drop the class of travel they use to save money. Airlines also have to explore possible **substitutes** for businesspeople travelling to meetings at all: the threats from the internet, from video conferencing and from mobile phones. Fundamentally, face-to-face communication is not found to be so necessary when times are hard, and technology is constantly improving its ability to simulate a one-on-one meeting.

T4 ANALYSIS TOOLS

It is difficult to stress enough the importance of fully understanding markets and customers. Much of this book has emphasised the 'look before you leap' philosophy of understanding and developing marketing activity before jumping into delivering it. The following tools address two of the most important aspects of marketing analysis: first, understanding markets and customers and getting to grips with the value that you offer customers, in comparison to their wants and desires and the competition; and second, the analysis of attractive market portfolios.

Customer value analysis

Do you know what your customers value about your products or offerings? It's probably not price – which would be the initial guess of many people. Only by fully understanding the value that customers see from your offering, what they actually seek and what your competitors are offering, can you position your products and begin to exploit market opportunities.

The following tool provides a framework for customer value analysis that you can use to assess how you perform on the key customer value criteria against competitors and customer ideals. Having identified up to eight key value criteria as perceived by customers, you should then rank both your performance and that of your competitors against them. Ideally you should use this as a customer engagement tool to rank the criteria using customer perceptions, but if that is not possible then you should consider all internal and external feedback in setting the ranking.

Fill out the columns as follows:

→ **Type**. The area each of the criteria primarily relates to: product features or attributes; process aspects in the way the product or service is delivered; people relationships or price.

→ **P**. The relative customer priority of each criterion.

→ **Us/Comp**. How well the business and competitors perform against the customer 'ideal': 10 is a perfect fit, while 0 is no fit at all.

→ **Status**. The status of the response to the analysis: Red indicates that immediate action is required as a competitor is performing significantly better on the most important customer criteria; Amber indicates that future action will probably be required; Green indicates no action is needed at this time.

These sheets are available to download from the Fast Track companion website at **www.Fast-Track-Me.com**.

Title		Issues	
Description		Risks	
Owner		Insights	
Update		Last save	

	CUSTOMER CRITERIA	TYPE	IDEAL PERFORMANCE	PRIORITY	US	COMP.	STATUS
A							
B							
C							
D							
E							
F							
G							
H							

Using this data, you can create a chart that demonstrates very visually how you and your competitors stack up against the value that customers are seeking from a purchase. Here is an example:

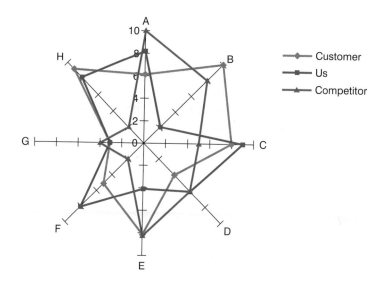

This customer value analysis activity can be quick and dirty, by talking to a handful of approachable customers, or more thorough, if you use formal market research. Either way, it means you get a better understanding of what your customers think and feel, on a scale of 1 to 10, about key attributes of your offering. This is shown by the blue line. You can then measure your business and how your competitors stack up, as demonstrated by the green and red lines.

If done properly, this analysis is invaluable for establishing and positioning value for customers and sustainable differentiation from competitors.

Portfolio analysis

Portfolios and their management are a key marketing skill that you and your team should master. While we have talked about portfolios in the broadest sense, they are most often used for analysing products and markets. Businesses need to identify, categorise and prioritise the markets that they aim to address and portfolio analysis is an important technique for achieving that.

Completing your own portfolio analysis

The following framework provides a useful tool for assessing market portfolios by understanding market attractiveness and competitive position. This helps you to collate the information you need for the portfolio analysis, as well as providing the basis for a structured analysis tool. First, fill in the information that will provide some background to the analysis, using the table and descriptions below:

	DESCRIPTION
Title	
Description	
Owner	
Markets and customers	
Products and services	
Key industry facts	

	PRODUCT NAME	DESCRIPTION	VALUE	SCORE
A				
B				
C				
D				
E				
F				
G				
H				

→ **Title.** What is the brief title for this industry analysis?

→ **Description.** What is the description of this industry or market segment?

→ **Owner.** Who is the person with overall responsibility for the analysis?

→ **Markets and customers.** What is the description of the market in terms of segments and type of company?

→ **Products and services.** What is the description of products and services being offered to the defined markets and customers?

→ **Key industry facts.** What are the key facts relating to this industry or segment? Consider the total number of customers and their total spend on the specified products and services.

→ **Product name.** What companies or products will be assessed as part of this portfolio?

→ **Description.** What is the scope of the company or product definition?

→ **Value.** What is the value, market share or size of each company or product?

→ **Score.** What is the relative importance of each product or business? Reflect on the overall value of each in terms of revenues or profit, and consider their relative strategic importance or relevance to the business.

After this introduction, you can now move on to filling in the detailed sections of the analysis, the first of which covers *market attractiveness*.

	MARKET ATTRACTIVENESS CRITERIA	INDICATOR	P
M1			
M2			
M3			
M4			
M5			
M6			
M7			
M8			

	P	A	B	C	D	E	F	G	H
		SCORE	SCORE	SCORE	SCORE	SCORE	SCORE	SCORE	SCORE
M1									
M2									
M3									
M4									
M5									
M6									
M7									
M8									

→ **Market attractiveness criteria**. What criteria reflect the attractiveness of a market? Consider what factors would affect market potential – e.g. growth, size, barriers to entry.

→ **Indicator**. What will indicate performance against each criterion?

→ **P**. What is the relative importance (priority) of each criterion? Identify the most important and assign it a score of 10, then assess each other criterion relative to this most important one. This value is then used as the first in the first column of the next table and is pre-populated in a spreadsheet (or the web tool at **www.Fast-Track-Me.com**).

→ **A score**. How does company or product A perform against each market attractiveness criterion? Score from 1 to 10, where 10 is the 'ideal'. Use the same scoring mechanism for each company, A to H.

Next, enter the information to assess the *competitive position* for each product or business.

	COMPETITIVE POSITIONING CRITERIA	INDICATOR	P
C1			
C2			
C3			
C4			
C5			
C6			
C7			
C8			

	P	A SCORE	B SCORE	C SCORE	D SCORE	E SCORE	F SCORE	G SCORE	H SCORE
C1									
C2									
C3									
C4									
C5									
C6									
C7									
C8									

→ **Competitive positioning criteria**. What criteria reflect competitiveness? Consider what factors would affect competitiveness – e.g. market share, capabilities.

→ **Indicator**. What will indicate performance against each criterion?

→ **P**. What is the priority or relative importance of each criterion? Identify the most important and assign it a score of 10, then assess each other criterion in relation to the most important. Again, enter this pre-populated field into the first column of the second table.

→ **A score.** How does company or product A perform against each competitive positioning criterion? Score from 1 to 10, where 10 is the 'ideal'. Use the same scoring mechanism for each company, A to H.

Finally, the summary captures the key details from the analysis.

	PRODUCT/COMPANY DESCRIPTION	MARKET SCORE	POSITION SCORE	VALUE	STATUS
A					
B					
C					
D					
E					
F					
G					
H					

→ **Product/company description.** What companies or products will be assessed as part of this portfolio?

→ **Market score.** What is the relative importance of each criterion?

→ **Position score.** What is the relative importance of each criterion?

→ **Value.** What is the value, market share or size of each company or product?

→ **Status.** What is the status of each offering, based on a combination of its competitive position and the attractiveness of the market?

The output from this toolkit would typically look like the following example (which shows a portfolio of five products). This kind of chart can be created manually by using the two sets of criteria for the two axes, but in reality it is best done on a spreadsheet or using the tool on the companion website (**www.Fast-Track-Me.com**).

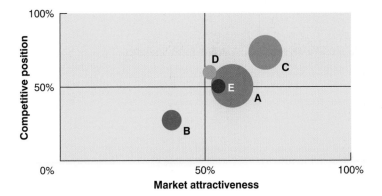

T5 MARKETING PROJECT CHECKLIST

What process can we follow to implement ideas?

There is no single right or wrong answer to this. The stages will vary enormously depending on the industry, the size of the business or the complexity of the project. Some projects or activities might not need a detailed checklist or project tracker, as they can be implemented quickly and simply following a brief meeting and a short list of agreed actions. However, if, for example, the target is to capture a 10 per cent market share by extending existing product offerings into a new vertical market, then a five-minute chat over lunch is probably insufficient. Spend an appropriate amount of time planning and, where possible, use simple checklists – such as the example overleaf to make sure everyone is following a common approach based on best practice.

What is a typical workplan?

The table overleaf reflects the generic tasks that would be included in each stage, from developing an idea to implementation. Here the description of each field is entered within the table; a blank version is available to download online at **www.Fast-Track-Me.com**.

The example here is fairly comprehensive and so might look a little daunting. Remember that not all fields will be applicable to all projects, and some will need to be adapted to suit your business and your specific needs. Go through them and decide where you need to take a shortcut or adapt the methodology to take account of your specific case and timescale constraints. Sometimes you simply have to go for it and leave a few stones unturned.

This template only shows the top-level workplan for the understand, develop, execute and review phases of the marketing process. For a significant programme these will be broken down into more detail at lower levels to provide a comprehensive plan of activity.

	OVERVIEW		STATUS
Title	Project name	Last update	When was the data last updated?
Description	Brief description of the project	Update	Short comment on the latest update from the project leader
Project leader	Name of the project leader	Status	What is the overall status of this project? (E.g. Red, Amber or Green: in the web-based tool this is automatically updated from lower levels)
Sponsor	Who is the primary internal (executive) sponsor for the project?	Budget	What is the agreed budget?
Company or team	Is the project associated with a specific team, group or client?	Spend	What is the actual current spend?
Programme	What programme is this project part of? (Projects are often grouped into programmes where there are complementary or common goals)	Budget variance	What is the current budget variance? (This might be calculated automatically)
Project type	What type or classification of project is this? (E.g. new product development, internal process improvement or market promotion: this can be useful for creating reports)	Scope changes	Number and audit of scope changes to the project (this is automated and audited in the web tool)
Period	In which time frame or business period is the project being planned, executed and delivered?	Issues and risks	How many issues and risks have been captured for the project? (Automated in the web tool)
Current phase	What is the current project phase?	Documents	How many documents are linked to the project? (Automated in the web tool)

		EXECUTIVE SUMMARY
A	Business context	What is the current situation and background information? (Capture information and facts that will influence and guide the project)
B	Business goal	Which business goal or goals does this project contribute to?
C	Objectives	What are the key objectives to be achieved?
D	Scope – in	What is the scope of the project? Specifically, what elements (deliverables or activities) should be included?
E	Scope – out	What elements are explicitly excluded?
F	Constraints and dependencies	What are the resources, timing and budgetary constraints, and what dependencies exist with other projects?

	IMPACT RATING	RATING		RISK RATING	RATING
I1	Valuable – what value will the project bring in monetary or other terms?	1–5	R1	Complexity – how complicated is the project relative to capabilities?	1–5
I2	Aligned – how well aligned is the project to current direction?	1–5	R2	Size – how big is the project relative to experience and overall resources?	1–5
I3	Strategic – does the project have enduing and strategic value?	1–5	R3	Novelty – what is the level of experience in implementing similar projects?	1–5
I4	Achievable – what is the likelihood of success?	1–5	R4	Control – to what extent do we have control over key aspects of the project? (Note 5 is low control and thus higher risk)	1–5

This analysis can then be used for prioritising projects in case of limited resources: select those that have high impact and low risk.

	WORKPLAN	OUTCOME OR DELIVERABLE	LINK TO TASKS	START DATE	TARGET CLOSE	ACTUAL CLOSE	STATUS
P1	Understand	Work breakdown of key tasks in the understand phase	Web link on tool to drill down to tasks				Red, Amber, Green
P2	Develop	Work breakdown of key tasks in the develop phase					
P3	Execute	Work breakdown of key tasks in the execute phase					
P4	Review	Work breakdown of key tasks in the review phase					

Finally, a summary is created at the end of the project as part of the review phase, to capture learning and assess the level of success.

	CLOSE-DOWN	STATUS	COMMENTS
1	Objectives	Red, Amber, Green	How well did the project deliver against objectives?
2	Timings		How well were project deadlines met?
3	Budget		Was the project delivered within the budget?
4	Resources		How well were project resources deployed?
5	Stakeholders		What was the feedback from stakeholders? How well were they engaged and satisfied?
6	Lessons learned		Link to lessons learned

THE FAST TRACK WAY

Take time to reflect

Within the Fast Track series, we cover a lot of ground quickly. Depending on your current role, company or situation, some ideas will be more relevant than others. Go back to your individual and team audits and reflect on the 'gaps' you have identified, and then take time to review each of the top ten tools and techniques and list of technologies.

Next steps

Based on this review, you will identify many ideas about how to improve your performance, but look before you leap: take time to plan your next steps carefully. Rushing into action is rarely the best way to progress unless you are facing a crisis. Think carefully about your own personal career development and that of your team. Identify a starting place and consider what would have a significant impact on performance and be easy to implement. Then make a simple to-do list with timings for completion.

Staying ahead

Finally, the fact that you have taken time to read and think hard about the ideas presented here suggests that you are already a professional in your chosen discipline. However, all areas of business leadership are changing rapidly and you need to take steps to stay ahead as a leader in your field. Take time to log in to the Fast Track web-resource, at **www.Fast-Track-Me.com**, and join a community of like-minded professionals.

Good luck!

OTHER TITLES IN THE FAST TRACK SERIES

This title is one of many in the Fast Track series that you may be interested in exploring. While each title works as a standalone solution, together they provide a comprehensive cross-functional approach that creates a common business language and structure. The series includes titles on the following:

→ Strategy

→ Innovation

→ Project management

→ Finance

→ Sales

GLOSSARY

above the line Paid-for advertising in mass media such as TV, press, radio and the web, often delivered through an advertising agency. See also *below the line*, *push promotion* and *pull promotion*

added value The increase in worth of a product or service as a result of a particular activity – in the context of marketing, the activity might be packaging or branding

adoption curve The phases through which consumers or the market as a whole move when adopting a new product or service: innovators, early adopters, early majority, late majority, laggards

ad tracking research The measurement of the effectiveness of an advertisement over time

advertising value equivalent (AVE) A commonly used PR measurement of the value of the space secured by PR executives had they bought that equivalent amount of space in advertising

advocacy advertising Advertising that expresses a viewpoint on a given issue, often on behalf an institution. Examples are to be found in anti-drink-driving campaigns

affiliate marketing A form of marketing or advertising used on the internet. Affiliate sites that serve web ads are paid according to results, normally per click

affinity marketing Marketing that targets affinity groups: individuals sharing common interests that predispose them towards a product. Also used to describe joint campaigns from disparate organisations that are non-competitive but have a particular interest in common

AIDA Attention, interest, desire, action: a model describing the process that advertising or promotion is intended to initiate in the mind of a prospective customer

AIUAPR Awareness, interest, understanding, attitudes, purchase, repeat purchase: a buying decision model

alliance An agreement between two companies in order to develop a new product or exploit a new market where risks and rewards are shared

ambush marketing A deliberate attempt by an organisation to associate itself with an event (often a sporting event) in order to gain some of the benefits associated with being an official sponsor without incurring the costs of sponsorship (for example, by advertising during broadcasts of the event)

Ansoff matrix A model that relates marketing strategy to general strategic direction. It maps product-market strategies – e.g. market penetration, product development, market development and diversification – on a matrix that shows new versus existing products along one axis and new versus existing markets along the other

asset-led marketing Marketing that uses product strengths such as the name and brand image to market both new and existing products. Marketing decisions are based on the needs of the consumer *and* the assets of the product

attribute testing A method of identifying customer or consumer preferences by asking them to rate a list of products or attributes using a common scale

awareness A measure of how many or what percentage of target customers are aware of a particular product or brand

B2B Business-to-business: a business that sells products or provides services to other businesses

B2C Business-to-consumer: a business that sells products or provides services to the end-user consumers

balanced scorecard A technique allowing a company to monitor and manage performance against defined objectives. Measurements might typically cover financial performance, customer value, internal business process, and people performance and development

banner adverts Adverts on web pages with a variety of sophistication and targeting methods, which are used to build brand awareness or drive traffic to the advertiser's own website. See also *affiliate marketing*

banner blindness The term used when website visitors ignore banner ads

BCG (Boston Consulting Group) matrix A model for product portfolio analysis. Products can be classified as: stars – high growth rate and high market share; cash cows – high market share and low growth rate; question marks – low market share in high growth rate markets; dogs – low market share and low growth rate

behaviouristic segmentation A method for dividing buyers into groups on the basis of their knowledge, attitude, use or response to a product

below the line Non-media advertising or promotion when no commission has been paid to the advertising agency. It includes direct mail, point of sale displays and giveaways. See also *above the line*, *push promotion* and *pull promotion*

benchmarking A method of comparing the performance of one company or process with others, including the market leader or best practice

benefit An attribute of a product or service expressed in terms of the positive impact it has on the user

best practice Processes, skills and systems that are considered to deliver optimum performance. These are often associated with market leaders

blogs/blogging The abbreviation of web logs, which are used by individuals or companies to express thoughts and opinions online. Businesses can use blogs as a marketing communication channel

brainstorming A method of generating new ideas on a particular topic within a group situation. The key is to make the initial list quickly without discussion before evaluating the list as a whole

brand The set of physical attributes of a product or service, including name, design and features, together with the surrounding beliefs, perceptions and expectations that distinguish one product or company from another in the minds of audiences

brand equity Essentially the value associated with a particular brand, either in the mind of the customer or sometimes in an accounting or business measurement sense

brand experience What the consumer learns and senses from contact with a brand

brand extension The process by which a company develops new products to be marketed under an existing brand name

brand management The process by which marketers attempt to optimise the marketing mix for a specific brand

brand ranking The rank order of brands by market share

brand value The value that a brand would be given if it was represented on a company balance sheet. It is what the brand is worth to the business and shareholders, which is sometimes defined as the net present value of cash flows from the brand minus those of an unbranded equivalent

breakthrough A fundamentally different idea or way of thinking that is clearly distinctive when compared with similar ideas

business case A formal analysis of a new idea to validate whether it will provide a satisfactory return on the investment required to make it happen

business intelligence tools Software tools that allow users to manipulate, interpret and display data through digital dashboards

business plan A strategic document showing cash flow, forecasts and direction of a company

business strategy The means by which a business works towards achieving its stated aims

buying behaviour The process that buyers go through when deciding whether or not to purchase goods or services. Buying behaviour can be influenced by a variety of external factors and motivations, including marketing activity

buying intent The likelihood that a consumer will purchase a product or service

buzz Buzz marketing uses word-of-mouth advertising: potential customers pass round information about a product. See also *viral marketing*

cannibalisation What happens when a new marketing channel or product 'steals' business from existing channels or products without adding new growth. This has to be taken into consideration when calculating the real return on investment of a new idea

category management Products are grouped and managed by strategic business unit categories. These are defined by how consumers views goods rather than by how they look to the seller, e.g. confectionery could be part of either a 'food' or a 'gifts' category and marketed depending on the category into which it's grouped

causal research Research that determines whether one variable causes or determines the value of another

cause-related marketing The partnership between a company or brand and a charity or 'cause', by which the charity benefits financially from the sale of specific products

channels The methods used by a company to communicate and interact with its customers

clicks-and-mortar A business that has both a physical and an online presence

click-stream A user's internet activity, including websites visited, length of time and actions during the visit

click-through The act of a user clicking on an internet advertisement that opens a link to the advertiser's website

co-branding Joint venture marketing under more than one brand name and possibly from different companies

comparative advertising Advertising that compares a company's product with that of competing brands. It must be used with caution to avoid accusations of misrepresentation from competitors

competitive advantage The product, proposition or benefit that puts a company ahead of its competitors

competitive intelligence Information about competitors that enables an organisation to gain competitive advantage. For example, this may relate to their strengths and weaknesses, or their plans for new product introductions

competitor analysis The formal analysis of a competitor, involving the review of their financial performance, as well as their strategy, operations, product lines and customer base

confusion marketing The controversial strategy of deliberately confusing the customer. Examples are alleged to be found in the telecommunications market, where pricing plans can be so complicated that it becomes impossible to make direct comparisons between competing offers

consumer The user of a product or service. This may or may not be the person who buys it

consumer behaviour The buying habits and buying patterns of consumers in the acquisition and use of goods and services

contextual marketing Marketing that occurs when a person is more likely to be interested in a product or service

contingency plan A plan to mitigate the effects of a potential problem, should it occur

conversion rate The percentage of the target audience that takes the desired action in response to a marketing campaign such as web or direct mail

core benefit proposition (CBP) The main benefit or value that customers will receive as a result of adopting a new idea

corporate reputation A complex mix of characteristics, such as ethos, identity and image, that go to make up a company's public personality. Corporate reputation hinges on investor confidence, unlike brand reputation which is contingent on customer confidence and is reflected in sales

corporate strategy The policies of a company with regard to its choice of businesses and customer groups

cost leadership The strategy of producing goods at a lower cost than one's competitors

cost per click (CPC) A specific type of cost-per-action programme, where advertisers pay for each time a user clicks on an ad or link

cost per thousand (CPT) A standard measurement used for determining the cost effectiveness for a specific medium. It compares the cost of the advertisement to the number of impressions to the target audience

critical success factor (CSF) A factor of a new idea or its implementation that is necessary for its successful introduction

crossing the chasm Successfully making the transition from the innovation stage of introducing a new idea to adoption by the mass market. The term 'chasm' relates to the risk of failure associated with an idea that has yet to prove its worth

customer acquisition cost (CAC) The total cost associated with acquiring a customer

customer lifetime value The value of a customer to a firm over the life of the customer–firm relationship

customer loyalty Feelings or attitudes that incline a customer either to return to a company, shop or outlet to purchase there again, or else to repurchase a particular product, service or brand

customer relationship management (CRM) The coherent management of contacts and interactions with customers. (This term is often used as if it is related purely to the use of IT, but IT should in fact be regarded as a facilitator of CRM.)

customer satisfaction The provision of goods or services that fulfil the customer's expectations in terms of quality and service, in relation to price paid

customer value analysis A structured approach to analysis of customer must-haves and wants, showing how a company performs against its competitors

cyber-stealth marketing Covert attempts using the internet to boost brand image, to make websites appear more popular than they are or to manipulate search engine listings

data mining The process of reviewing and analysing data for the purpose of identifying common characteristics that may be useful for other purposes

Data Protection Act A law that makes organisations responsible for protecting the privacy of personal data. The current act (Data Protection Act 1998) is the UK's response to the requirement to implement national legislation in accordance with the European Directive 95/46/EC

database marketing How customer information is stored and used for targeting marketing activities. Information can be a mixture of what is gleaned from previous interactions with the customer and what is available from outside sources. See also *customer relationship management*

decision making unit (DMU) The team of people in an organisation who make the final buying decision

demand and supply Demand is the desire for a product at the market price; supply is the quantity available at that price

demographic data Information describing and segmenting a population in terms of age, sex, income and so on, which can be used to target marketing campaigns

differentiation The distinct attributes or features of a product or service that help to provide a source of advantage over competitors

direct mail The delivery of an advertising or promotional message to customers or potential customers by mail

direct marketing All activities that make it possible to offer goods or services or to transmit other messages to a segment of the population by post, telephone, email or other direct means

direct response advertising (DRA) Advertising incorporating a contact method such as a phone number, address and enquiry form, website identifier or email address, with the intention of encouraging the recipient to respond directly to the advertiser by requesting more information, placing an order and so on

discounted cash flow (DCF) A method of estimating an investment's current value based on the discounting of projected future revenues and costs. The further into the future the flow occurs, the more heavily it will be discounted

diversification An increase in the variety of goods and services produced by an individual enterprise or conglomerate. It may be encouraged, either by business owners or by governments, in order to reduce the risk of relying on a narrow range of products

DRIP framework Differentiate, reinforce, inform, persuade: a marketing communications model

early adopters Customers who will use their own judgement to adopt a new product or service very early on in its life cycle

e-commerce or e-marketing Marketing conducted electronically, usually over the internet

economic value add (EVA) The financial value associated with a new idea – taking into account life cycle costs and benefits

efficient consumer response (ECR) Having the right product in the right place at the right price with the right promotions. See also *category management* – with its emphasis on how products look to the customer, category management is seen as an integral part of achieving ECR

emotional selling preposition (ESP) The unique associations established by consumers with particular products. For example, the emotional response to certain car brands ensures their continual success, even though other makers may offer superior performance at the same price

endorsement An affirmation, usually from a celebrity, that a product is good

ethical marketing Marketing that takes account of the moral aspects of decisions

exit strategy A plan for withdrawing a product or service from a market at a point in time. This might be due to a limited market or declining performance. This term also refers to a planned sale of a business by its founders

export marketing The marketing of goods or services to overseas customers

external analysis A study of the external marketing environment, including factors such as customers, competition and social change

FAST marketing Focused advertising sampling technique: an approach concentrating promotions into a short space of time to saturate the market

Fax Preference Service (FPS) A database of business and individual telecoms subscribers who have elected not to receive unsolicited direct marketing faxes

field marketing The practice of sending representatives or agents to retail outlets with a view to building brand and supporting sales. They may, for example, conduct in-store promotions, set up point-of-sale displays and ensure that products are displayed to best advantage

first to market The first product or service in a new emerging market. These products will often gain what is called first mover or prime mover advantage

FMCG Fast moving consumer goods – such as packaged food, beverages, toiletries and tobacco

focus group A market research method where a group of participants is brought together to provide feedback on ideas, products and services

forecasting The calculation of future events and performance

four Ps See *marketing mix*

franchising The selling of a licence by the owner (franchisor) to a third party (franchisee), permitting the sale of a product or service for a specified period. In business format franchising the agreement will involve a common brand and marketing format

gap analysis An assessment of the difference between the current performance and the desired or target performance

grey marketing (also called parallel importing) The illicit sale of imported products contrary to the interests of a holder of a trademark, patent or copyright in the country of sale

guerrilla marketing Unconventional marketing that is intended to get maximum results from minimal resources. It often targets small and specialised customer groups in such a way that bigger companies will not find it worthwhile to retaliate

impression An instance of an online ad being loaded on to a page

inducements Incentives that are offered to overcome resistance to purchase – for example, 'special offers' or money-back guarantees

industrial marketing The marketing of industrial products

infiltration marketing When marketers join chat rooms posing as ordinary users in order to spread marketing messages, usually as personal endorsements

influencer A person influential and carrying weight in making the final buying decision

internal analysis The study of a company's internal marketing resources in order to assess opportunities, strengths or weaknesses

internal customers The employees within an organisation who are viewed as consumers of a product or service provided by another part of the organisation – products or services that the employees need to do their own work. For example, the marketing department could be internal customers of the IT department

internal marketing The process of eliciting support for a company and its activities among its own employees, in order to encourage them to promote its goals. This process can happen at a number of levels, from increasing awareness of individual products or marketing campaigns, to explaining overall business strategy

joint venture A business entity or partnership formed by two or more parties for a specific purpose – for example, Virgin Mobile is a 50:50 joint venture company between Virgin Group and Deutsche Telekom's One 2 One

key account management Account management as applied to a company's most important customers

key success factors (KSFs) Those factors that are a necessary condition for success in a given market. That is, a company that does poorly on one of the factors critical to success in its market is certain to fail

keyword buying When advertisers pay for links to their websites to appear on internet search engines alongside search results, sometimes as 'sponsored links', based on keywords entered into the search engine. See also *search marketing*

lock-in The ability of companies to ensure their customers do not switch to competitors (i.e. mobile phone companies)

LTV Long term or life time value

macro environment The external factors that affect a company's planning and performance and are beyond its control – for example, socio-economic, legal and technological change. See also *micro environment*

Mailing Preference Service (MPS) A database of individual home addresses where the occupiers have elected not to receive unsolicited direct (marketing) mail

market challenger A firm attempting to gain market leadership through marketing efforts – see also *market follower* and *market leader*

market development The process of growing sales by offering existing products (or new versions of them) to new customer groups (as opposed to simply attempting to increase the company's share of current markets)

market entry The launch of a new product into a new or existing market. A different strategy is required depending on whether the product is an early or late entrant to the market; the first entrant usually has an automatic advantage, while later entrants need to demonstrate that their products are better, cheaper and so on

market follower A firm that is happy to follow the leaders in a marketplace without challenging them, perhaps taking advantages of opportunities created by leaders without the need for much marketing investment of its own. See also *market challenger* and *market leader*

marketing audit The scrutiny of an organisation's existing marketing system to ascertain its capabilities, strengths and weaknesses.

marketing communications All the methods used by a firm to communicate with its customers and prospective customers

marketing information Any information used or required to support marketing decisions – often drawn from a computerised 'marketing information system'

marketing metrics Measurements that help with the quantification of marketing performance, such as market share, advertising spend and response rates elicited by advertising and direct marketing

marketing mix The unique blend of attributes, including products, pricing, promotion and distribution, targeting a specific group of people

marketing myopia A lack of vision on the part of companies, particularly in failing to spot customers' desires through excessive product focus. The term derives from a seminal article by Theodore Levitt published in *Harvard Business Review* in 1960

marketing orientation A business strategy whereby customers' needs and wants, as identified by the marketing function, determine corporate direction

marketing planning The selection and scheduling of activities to support the company's chosen marketing strategy or goals. See also *marketing strategy*

marketing strategy The set of objectives, approaches and broad methods that an organisation allocates to its marketing function in order to support the overall corporate strategy

market leader The seller of the product or service with the largest market share in its field. See also *market challenger* and *market follower*

market penetration The attempt to grow the business by obtaining a larger market share in an existing market. See *market share* and *market development*

market research (or marketing research) The gathering and analysis of data relating to marketplaces or customers, including market size and growth, segmentation, customer decision criteria and competition; any research that leads to more market knowledge and better-informed decision making

market segmentation The division of the marketplace into distinct sub-groups or segments, each characterised by particular tastes and requiring a specific marketing mix. See also *marketing mix*

market share Sales of a particular product, service or firm as a percentage of the overall market

market testing The formal evaluation of a new idea with customers, either within a controlled environment such as a focus group or within a pilot market

marketing The management process responsible for identifying, anticipating and satisfying customer requirements profitably

mass marketing Untargeted marketing which promotes products to many groups of buyers with undifferentiated approaches

McKinsey's seven S's of management (or 7-S model) A framework for considering business strategy with reference to seven interrelated aspects of the organisation: systems, structure, skills, style, staff, strategy and shared values.

MDSS Marketing decision support system

merger/acquisition A merger is the formation of one company from two existing companies; an acquisition is one company acquiring control of another by purchase of a majority shareholding

micro environment The immediate context of a company's operations, including such elements as suppliers, customers and competitors. See also *macro environment*

models (or marketing models) Graphical representations of a process designed to aid in understanding and/or forecasting. Computerised models allow the simulation of scenarios based on different assumptions about changes to the macro environment and micro environment. See also *macro environment* and *micro environment*

new product development (NPD) The process for developing a new product from initial concept or idea to in-market commercialisation

niche marketing The marketing of a product to a small and well-defined segment of the marketplace

offensive marketing A competitive marketing strategy designed to win market share away from other players in the market

opportunity cost The lost benefits of indirect costs that are associated with the adoption of an idea or programme. For example, developing one product may prohibit the development of an alternative product

opt-in When users give marketers explicit permission to send them information

opt-out When users do not give marketers explicit permission to send them information

organic growth/development A company's expansion by the growth of its activities and ploughing back of profits, rather than by mergers/acquisitions. See also *merger/acquisition*

OTS Opportunities to see

packaging Material used to protect

goods; also an opportunity to present the brand and logo

page view The same as a 'hit' (on a web page)

payment by results (PBR) Remuneration of an employee or service provider according to productivity or other measure of performance

peer to peer (P2P) marketing The technique of encouraging customers to promote your product to one another, particularly on the internet. An example might be a website that offers users a discount on products in return for recruiting new customers for the site. See also *word of mouth* and *viral marketing*

penetration The percentage of the target market that purchased the brand at least once during the period

performance indicators Measures of performance associated with an idea. They should be SMART: specific to the idea, measurable, agreed, realistic and time-bound

permission marketing Marketing to customers who have opted-in

personal data Data related to a living individual who can be identified from the information, including any expression of opinion about the individual

personal selling One-to-one communication between a seller and prospective purchaser

PESTEL Political, economic, social, technological, environmental and legal: a framework for viewing the macro environment. See also *macro environment*

physical evidence The elements of the marketing mix that customers can actually see or experience when they use a service, and which contribute to the perceived quality of the service, e.g. the physical evidence of a retail bank could include the state of the branch premises, as well as the delivery of the banking service itself

PIMS Profit Impact of Marketing Strategies: a database supplying data

such as environment, strategy, competition and internal data with respect to 3,000 businesses. This data can be used for benchmarking purposes

podcast/podcasting The broadcasting of multimedia files to iPods or other similar devices. Subscribers are able to view or listen to podcasts online

point of sale (POS) (also called point of purchase) The location, usually within a retail outlet, where the customer decides whether to make a purchase

pop-up An automatically launched internet advertisement that appears in a small window in front of another web page

Porter's five forces An analytic framework developed by Michael Porter to analyse the current trends and drivers in an industry. The five forces that the model uses to analyse businesses and industries are: buyers, suppliers, substitutes, new entrants and rivals

portfolio (and portfolio analysis) The set of products or services that a company decides to develop and market. Portfolio analysis is the process of comparing the contents of the portfolio to see which products or services are the most promising and deserving of further investment, and which should be discontinued. Can also refer to groups of ideas, projects or markets, as well as products and services

portfolio map A graphical representation of a portfolio of ideas or projects, etc., used to identify the relative strengths and weaknesses of each item. Axes will vary, but most common will be market attractiveness and competitive position

positioning The creation of an image for a product or service in the minds of customers, both specifically to that item and in relation to competitive offerings

PPC Pay-per-click

PPL Pay-per-lead

PPS pay-per-sale

PR See *public relations*

product development See *new product development*

product life cycle The stages that a new product will go through: introduction, growth, maturity and decline

product line A group of products or services with similar characteristics or attributes, possibly sold under the same brand

product placement The use of a product or service within a television or radio programme, or a film: an example would be the appearance of a leading coffee brand on a table in *Eastenders*. There are strict guidelines as to the payments that can be given for such appearances

Professional Marketing Standards The grid of marketing competencies required by the Chartered Institute of Marketing (CIM) to achieve business aims. CIM's new syllabus structure is mapped out against each marketing level as identified in the grid

promotional mix The components of an individual promotional campaign, which are likely to include advertising, personal selling, public relations, direct marketing, packaging and sales promotion

public relations The function or activity that aims to establish and protect the reputation of a company or brand, and to create mutual understanding between the organisation and the segments of the public with whom it needs to communicate

pull promotion Pull promotion, in contrast to push promotion, addresses the customer directly with a view to getting them to demand the product, and hence 'pull' it down through the distribution chain. It focuses on advertising and above-the-line activities. See also *push promotion*

push promotion Push promotion relies on the next link in the distribution chain – e.g. a wholesaler or retailer – to 'push' out products to the customer. It revolves around sales promotions – such as price reductions and point-of-

sale displays – and other below-the-line activities. See also *sales promotion*

qualitative research A structured approach to conducting market research, working with consumers (individually or in groups) to ascertain their needs. This helps those in the marketing and product development teams to understand why consumers buy certain products and services

quantitative research Market research that concentrates on statistics and other numerical data, gathered through opinion polls, customer satisfaction surveys and so on. See also *qualitative research*

R&D Research and development

reference group A group with which the customer identifies in some way, and whose opinions and experiences influence the customer's behaviour. For example, a sports fan might buy a brand of equipment used by a favourite team

relationship marketing Marketing that helps companies develop long-term relationships with its customers

repositioning A strategic change for the brand, possibly in the consumers' perception of the brand

return on investment (ROI) The value that an organisation derives from investing

return on marketing investment (ROMI) The value that an organisation derives from investing in marketing

risk management The process of mitigating the impact of identified risks. Actions will be preventive (proactive action taken to prevent the risk occurring) or contingent (reactive action taken to minimise the impact if it does occur)

sales promotion A range of techniques used to engage the purchaser and drive short-term sales. These may include discounting, coupons, guarantees, free gifts, competitions, vouchers, demonstrations, bonus commission and sponsorship

sampling Small quantities of product given out to prospective buyers

satisfaction surveys A structured process for capturing feedback from customers in order to identify their overall level of satisfaction with the product or service that has been provided. Unfortunately, these surveys are often not a good predictor of future intentions to purchase

search engine optimisation (SEO) The process of choosing targeted keyword phrases related to a site, and ensuring that the site places well when those keyword phrases are part of a web search

search marketing Promoting a company's website using internet search engines. This can be either by getting a company website listed in search results (unpaid) or as a listing on the same web page as the search results (paid)

segmentation The process of dividing a large market into smaller groups. Each sub-group will have similar characteristics, and will therefore simplify the process of analysis and targeting

sensitivity analysis An assessment of the impact of changing a single variable on the overall performance or result

seven Ss See *McKinsey's seven Ss*

share of voice (SOV) The total percentage that you possess of the particular niche, market or audience you are targeting

shareholder value The worth of a company from the point of view of its shareholders. Maximising shareholder value is a common objective for business management

skimming Setting the original price high in the early stages of the product life cycle in an attempt to get as much profit as possible before prices are driven down by increasing competition

SMART objectives A simple acronym used to set objectives. SMART stands for: specific (what do you want to achieve?), measurable (what will be the value from investing in the project?), agreed (are the objectives agreed as well as achievable?), realistic (can you realistically achieve the objectives with the resources you have?) and time bound (when do you want to achieve the set objectives?)

SME Small to medium-sized enterprise. The exact size is variously defined: according to one EU definition, an SME must employ under 250 people, have either a turnover of less than €40 million or net balance sheet assets of less than €27 million, and not be more than 25 per cent owned by a larger company

spam Unsolicited email, often advertisements, sent to a very large number of recipients

spin The attempt to manipulate the depiction of news or events in the media through artful public relations – a term often used with derogatory connotations

sponsorship Marketing that seeks to establish a deeper association and integration between a business and its target audiences, often by supporting an event (sporting or cultural) or activity

strategic partnering An alliance or partnership between two organisations to improve their operational processes, create new products or exploit new markets

strategy The future vision and direction as well as the basis on which an organisation or team will compete or differentiate itself, its products and services, and its target markets and customers

supply chain The network of suppliers, manufacturers and distributors involved in the production and delivery of a product

SWOT analysis A method of analysis that examines a company's strengths, weaknesses, opportunities and threats. It is often used as part of the development process for a marketing plan, or to feed the results of a marketing audit back into a revised plan

target market The group of customers or consumers that is most likely to buy the product, or that represents the most significant strategic potential

targeting The use of market segmentation to select and address a key group of potential purchasers

telemarketing The marketing of a product or service over the telephone, typically outbound where customers are called with promotions, but it can also be used for research

Telephone Preference Service (TPS) A database of business and individual telecoms subscribers who have elected not to receive unsolicited direct marketing calls

test market A market of limited scope that is used to test a new product. It needs to be small enough to mitigate the risk of failure, but it also needs to reflect the target market so that results will guide implementation

through the line A combination of above-the-line and below-the-line communications programmes involving advertising and other promotional approaches such as direct mail

time to market The time taken to develop a new idea from concept to implementation or initial sales in the market. For some organisations, a faster time to market will provide a source of advantage

trade marketing Marketing to the retail and distributive trades

umbrella brand A broadly based brand that has under it sub-brands

unique selling preposition (USP) The benefit that a product or service can deliver to a customer that is not offered by any competitor: one of the fundamentals of effective marketing and business

VALS Values and lifestyles: the categorisation of people according to their way of living, using groupings such as belongers, achievers, emulators, I-am-me, experiential, socially conscious, survivors, sustainers and integrators

value chain As an idea or product moves through each stage of its development from idea to implementation, value is added. The value chain identifies each step and relative value added

value proposition A simple statement that describes the value a product or service gives to the customer or consumer. The word 'value' implies that it will describe benefits (possibly measured in financial terms) and not features or attributes

viral marketing Marketing that leverages customers to promote a company's products or services. Common techniques include using email messages, jokes, web addresses, film clips and games that get forwarded on electronically by recipients

virtual team A team working towards a common purpose but not located in the same facility, often using technology to work remotely

voice of the customer (VOC) An understanding of the must-haves and wants of different customer or consumer groups and the relevance of that to the organisation and individual teams

V-SAFE Generic criteria used to screen and prioritise new ideas: V = value to the organisation in terms of financial impact; S = suitable given the current situation and strategy; A = acceptable to the differing stakeholders impacted; F = feasible given current resource and budget constraints; and E = enduring beyond the current time period

Web 2.0 Second generation of web applications and web usage, including social networking, brought about by technology and the availability of network connectivity

window of opportunity The period of time during which a new idea or product can be launched successfully

word of mouth (WOM) marketing A form of viral marketing, generally one of the most effective forms of marketing

INDEX

Page numbers in **bold** relate to entries in the Glossary.